designer
style
handbags

designer style handbags

TECHNIQUES AND PROJECTS FOR UNIQUE, FUN, AND ELEGANT DESIGNS FROM CLASSIC TO RETRO

SHERRI HAAB

WATSON-GUPTILL PUBLICATIONS
New York

First published in 2005 by Watson-Guptill Publications,
a division of VNU Business Media, Inc.,
770 Broadway, New York, NY 10003
www.wgpub.com

All projects by Sherri Haab.
All photography by Dan Haab.

Information about the history of handbags (pages 9–10) provided by
the Fashion Accessories Shippers Association, Inc., and used by per-
mission. All rights reserved.

Library of Congress Cataloging-in-Publication Data
Haab, Sherri.
  Designer style handbags : techniques and projects for unique, fun, and
elegant designs from classic to retro / By Sherri Haab.
      p. cm.
  Includes index.
  ISBN 0-8230-1288-3 (alk. paper)
  1. Handbags. I. Title.

  TT667.H22 2005
  646.4'8--dc22

                              2005001346

Senior Aquisitions Editor: Joy Aquilino
Editor: Michelle Bredeson
Designer: Alexandra Maldonado
Production Manager: Ellen Greene

Manufactured in China

First printing, 2005

1 2 3 4 5 6 7 8 9 / 13 12 11 10 09 08 07 06 05

When using cutting tools and other suggested products,
readers are strongly cautioned to follow manufacturers'
directions, to heed warnings, and to seek prompt med-
ical attention for an injury. In addition, readers are
advised to keep all potentially harmful supplies away
from children.

acknowledgments

To my husband, Dan, thank you for the beautiful photographs and hours of hard work.

Thank you Michelle and Rachel for your great ideas and help with modeling.

Thanks to my friends and family for encouraging me along the way with helpful suggestions and project ideas.

Many thanks to the editorial and design staff at Watson-Guptill for the hard work and dedication to this book.

And thanks to the manufacturers who supplied product and technical support for the projects in this book.

contents

no-sew & embellished bags 84

introduction

I can still remember the first purse I made. I was about six years old and had a fascination for cool boxes, bottles, and small containers. I was always quick to rescue discarded items before they went out to the trash. To me they were like presents, art projects waiting to happen. On one particular occasion, my father threw out a small rectangular box. It had probably held a new doorknob or lightbulb, but to me it was a purse. I figured out how to fashion a handle out of string, and voilà—instant fashion! A purse any six-year-old would be happy to parade around with. I filled it with, what else, candy.

A treasured family photo provides the inspiration for a one-of-a-kind handbag made from a cigar box (page 86).

The next purse I recall was a gift from my aunt. This time it was a real purse. She made my sister and me identical red shoulder bags. These bags were well-worn and much loved, as evidenced by family photos. We looked like proud little soldiers sporting red quilted straps across our chests. I can't remember what we filled them with, but once again, I'm sure candy was involved.

A handbag is a time capsule of a woman's life, housing Barbie dolls and candy at age six, maturing to first checkbooks and pictures of friends. Later in life, these items are replaced by credit cards, a cell phone, and a flurry of receipts. No doubt a handbag is a commentary on what is going on in each stage of a woman's life.

The forms and functions of handbags haven't changed much throughout history. The first "handbags"—sacks filled with pomanders, flint, and money—were actually carried by men and hung from the waist. By the fifteenth century, women began carrying purses as well. These sacks were often ornamented with gold or embroidery to reflect the prosperity of the wearer.

By the end of the 1600s, women began wearing purses under their skirts, and men began carrying their possessions in the pockets of their breeches. Over the next couple of centuries purses came in and out of hiding, depending on styles of dresses. Some dresses, such as hobble skirts, which came into fashion at the turn of the twentieth century, could not accommodate a pocket, so women began carrying large bags on long strings or chains.

Handbags have remained in fashion since the 1920s, as both functional items and as a reflection of personal style. Around that time, innovative materials, such as celluloid, plastic, wood, and leather, began to be used to make designer bags, and designers created trademark designs that are still in vogue today. Purses and handbags crafted by today's designers are as innovative and artistic as they ever were.

A stylish bag is a fashion accessory that even the most conservative woman can indulge in. Designer and "novelty" handbags, seen on the arms of popular celebrities, are all the rage these days. Making your own designer handbags is inexpensive and provides a means of artistic expression as well as function. Best of all, handbags are easy to make. It's very satisfying to whip one together in an afternoon to wear with a special outfit that evening. If you make one for a gift, it's sure to be a welcome one. It's no wonder handbags have and always will be a girl's favorite fashion accessory.

Once you learn the basic method for making a classic fabric tote (page 28), you can vary the fabric, handles, and other details to create an endless number of original designs.

getting
started

Handbags are surprisingly easy to make, even if you don't have a lot of crafting or sewing experience. You can start one in an afternoon and use it that evening. Having all the right materials and tools on hand will make any project quicker and easier.

choosing fabrics

Selecting the right fabric can mean everything when designing the perfect bag. Fabric and quilting stores offer a variety of apparel fabrics, faux leathers and furs, upholstery fabrics, felt, and other materials you can use for making handbags. If you can't find exactly what you're looking for, try shopping online. There are reputable shops on the Internet that offer novelty and hard-to-find fabrics.

One great thing about making handbags is that you don't need a lot of fabric. Remnant pieces are usually large enough to make a bag or purse, and remnant bins at fabric stores are a great source for fabrics sold at discounted prices. Look in your closet or shop thrift stores for fabrics that can be recycled to make handbags. You can make a great retro-style purse with fabric from an old coat or a vintage housedress.

When choosing a fabric for your project, consider the following:

WEIGHT OF THE FABRIC

If you want a sturdier body for your bag you might choose leather, oilcloth, or upholstery fabric. Consider lightweight fabrics, such as cotton or linen, for handbags with a delicate design.

COLOR, PATTERN & TEXTURE

Handbag designs mirror current trends in fashion. Use color, pattern, and texture to coordinate with fashion and reflect the mood of the season. Brightly colored fabrics, floral cottons, and crisp pastels, bring to mind the youthful freshness of spring. Richly textured jewel tones or subdued colors lend a sophisticated look that's perfect to pair with warm knits, classic black, or formal evening wear.

Heavier, woven fabrics and subdued colors go well with winter and evening wear.

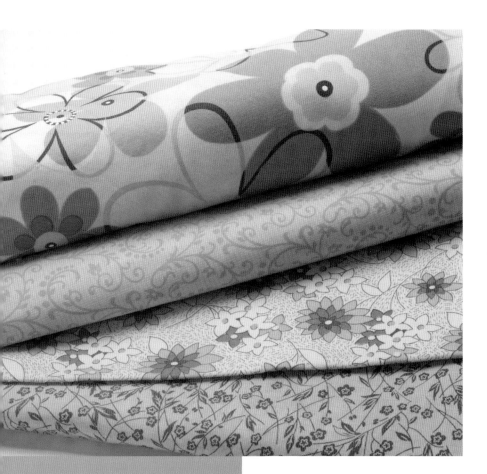

Crisp, lightweight fabrics in pale shades are perfect to pair with spring and summer fashions.

STYLE & FORM

Heavier fabrics are better suited for a simple shape or large bag, whereas lighter fabrics provide the right look for a woven or quilted design. Heavy fabric would be difficult to manage when making a bag with a lot of soft gathers. On the other hand, you might come up with a wonderful variation by breaking the rules and trying something unexpected.

CARE & CLEANING

Take care to read the cleaning instructions on the bolt of fabric you are considering. Make sure the fabric is compatible with the utility of the bag you want to make. Washable fabrics should be laundered before beginning bag construction. Some fabrics, especially upholstery fabrics, require dry cleaning.

IRONING

Pressing seams and sections of fabric as you construct a purse or bag will make it easier to make a neat, well-shaped finished piece. A press cloth will help to protect synthetic fabrics, leather, suede, ribbon, and other delicate materials from the heat of the iron. Some ribbons and polyester fibers are especially prone to damage and will melt or warp if ironed with direct heat or if the heat is set too high. If you don't have a press cloth, plain cotton fabric or an old pillowcase works just as well.

HOW THE BAG IS CONSTRUCTED

Consider how the bag will be sewn or fastened together. Some fabrics and materials require supplies and techniques specific to the fabric. Make sure you use the correct needle, machine setting, or stabilizer (see page 25) needed for certain fabrics. Vinyl and leather are examples of materials that require a little extra consideration for successful bag construction.

linings & interlinings

Linings and interlinings add shape and stability to a finished handbag, and there are many options available depending on the type of bag you are making. Lining fabric finishes the inside of the bag, and also adds support. The interlining is the support or structure between the main body fabric and the lining fabric.

LINING FABRICS

A lining gives a handbag a finished, professional look and hides the seams and raw edges inside the bag. The lining fabric also provides an added aesthetic appeal to the bag. For most of the projects in this book, the lining is a mirror image of the (outer) body of the handbag or purse; simply use the same pattern for both sections. You can make the lining with fabric that is equal in weight to the body, especially if you are making a reversible design. Otherwise, the lining fabric should be lighter in weight than the fabric for the body of the bag to prevent adding excess bulk. Choose a coordinating or neutral fabric for the lining.

Another consideration is the weave or texture of the fabric. Using lining fabric

Choose lining fabrics that coordinate with the main fabric of the bag. Here I show several possible pairings.

with a smooth tight weave will make it easier to keep the inside of the bag clean.

Additions to the lining will add function to a bag or purse. Sew a pocket for a cell phone or a loop for hanging keys onto the lining inside the purse before beginning bag construction.

INTERLINING

Interlining is an extra layer of support sandwiched between the lining and outer fabric of the bag. It gives support to the bag, allowing the sides to hold a shape without collapsing or sagging. There are different types of interlinings to choose from: interfacing, buckram, and quilt batting.

INTERFACING is used in clothing construction, most commonly to shape collars and belts. It is available in light, medium, and heavy weights. Most of the projects in this book that call for interfacing use the heavyweight, iron-on type. Trim the interfacing to remove the seam allowances before ironing to the wrong side of the fabric. This gives you one less seam to trim, reducing the bulk.

BUCKRAM is a rigid woven material used for making hats. Use this type of interlining when you want an extra stiff bag that will stand on its own. Buckram can be substituted when interfacing is called for in a project. To work with buckram, cut the pieces using the same pattern as the body of the bag. Baste the buckram to the wrong side of the outer fabric, stitching around the edges of the fabric, before beginning bag construction. Trim away the seam allowance of the buckram close to the stitching to remove bulk. Continue to construct the bag as directed in the pattern.

QUILT BATTING adds a layer of thickness to the bag and also acts as a support. Handbags made with batting will have a wonderful tactile appeal. Iron-on batting, which is also called fusible fleece, makes an excellent interlining. Fusible fleece should be ironed to the wrong side of the outer fabric before beginning bag construction.

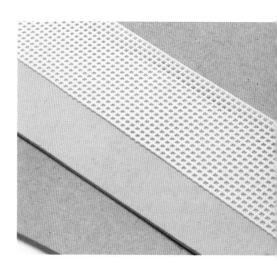

Cardboard, bookbinding board, and plastic canvas can all be used to add support to the bottom of a bag. Cut the piece the same size as the base of the bag and slip it into the bag between the lining and outside fabric.

BASE SUPPORTS

Several materials can be used to make a firm base to stabilize the bottom of a bag. Plastic canvas is a grid that resembles needlepoint fabric. Cut the canvas to fit and place it between the lining and fabric at the bottom of the bag to add a structure to the base. Heavy cardboard or bookbinding board can also be used in the same fashion. For large bags, or a stronger base, you can use pressed particle board.

The type of interlining you use depends on the form and construction of the bag you are making. From top to bottom: interfacing, quilt batting, and buckram.

handles & straps

Handles for handbags were once very difficult to come by, as they were available only to commercial manufacturers. Now with the rise in popularity of crafting handbags, many of these items are sold in craft and variety stores and online. There are wood, plastic, bamboo, and beaded handles in a variety of styles. Choose one that matches your design or combine craft materials, such as wire and beads, to make your own handles.

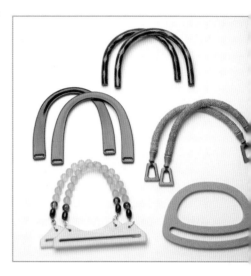

MAKING FABRIC STRAPS

Fabric can be used to make straps to match a fabric bag. This is an economical way to use up the leftover fabric scraps after cutting the bag pieces. You can make matching straps using the same fabric as the body of your bag or use contrasting fabric to complement a design. Be sure to use interfacing to add body to the straps.

To make a strap, cut a strip of the main purse fabric and reinforce it with interfacing. Cut the fabric as long and a little more than twice as wide as you want the finished strap. Fold the fabric and interfacing in half lengthwise with right sides together and stitch the long edge closed. Turn the handle right side out, press, and stitch the ends to the sides of the purse.

With all the styles of purchased handles available, it's easy to find one that fits the style and shape of the purse you are creating. The handle is as important as the fabric, so choose one that makes a statement.

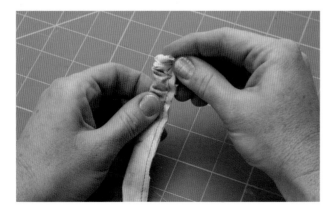

Use a safety pin to help turn a narrow fabric handle right side out after sewing. Attach the pin to one end and feed it through.

Pull the safety pin all the way through until the strap is right side out.

HARDWARE

Metal loops, either round or square, can be used to attach handles to a bag. Some purchased loops have a removable peg that allows you to choose which handle to add. Loop a fabric tab through the metal hardware. Sew the fabric tabs to the sides of the bag with the metal hardware pieces attached. After the bag is finished, add the purchased handle and replace the peg, screwing it into place.

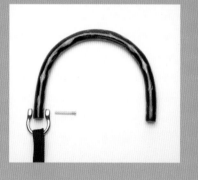

Cording, ribbon, braided trims, chain, wire, and plastic-coated cable can all be used to fashion a handle or strap for a handbag. Choose a material that coordinates with the design and function of the bag.

CORD & RIBBON STRAPS

Purchased cording, ribbon, and braided trims, found in fabric and craft stores, can be used as straps. If the cord or trim you are using is thin, braid several cords together to create a bulkier strap. Cords and trim are available in natural fibers, like cotton, or in a variety of synthetic fibers. Use hem sealant or white glue to prevent the ends of the cord from fraying before attaching the strap to the purse.

WIRE & CABLE HANDLES

Wire and plastic-coated cable make interesting alternatives to fabric or cord straps. Sturdy wire is available in craft or hardware stores. Thread beads with large holes onto the wire to make a stylish handle to complement a purse design. Plastic-coated jewelry wire, such as Tigertail, is very strong and is a good choice for flexible beaded straps, especially for small purses with long straps.

closures & fasteners

Depending on the design of your bag, you have several options for the type of closure you use. A stylish button can double as a decorative focal point as well as a functional closure. Other fasteners may be merely functional and hidden inside the bag. Many types of fasteners originally designed for clothing work equally well for handbag construction.

BUTTON & LOOP

To add a simple button closure, stitch a large button to the front of the purse with heavy-duty thread. Sew a cord loop to the opposite side of the purse or to the flap. Sew the loop between the lining and main fabric to hide the ends of the loop. The cord can then be looped over the button to hold the purse closed or the flap down.

MAGNETIC SNAPS

Magnetic snaps are a favorite among handbag designers because they are strong and will give your finished purse a polished look. Make sure you reinforce your fabric with extra interfacing or thin cardboard to support the snap and prevent tearing.

1. To apply a magnetic snap, first separate the magnetic snap pieces to attach one to each side of the lining panels of the purse so that the purse snaps closed inside. Add the snaps before stitching the lining into place inside the purse to hide the back side of the snaps. Mark slits on the reinforced fabric corresponding to the prongs of the snaps. Cut through the markings with a seam ripper.

2. Slip the prongs through the slits.

3. Replace the metal cover piece and bend the prongs over to hold. An alternative method is to add the magnetic snaps after the purse is finished by using small reinforced fabric tabs. Attach the snaps to the tabs, using the same method described above and then sew or glue the tabs in place inside the finished purse.

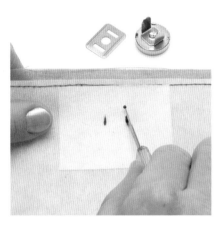

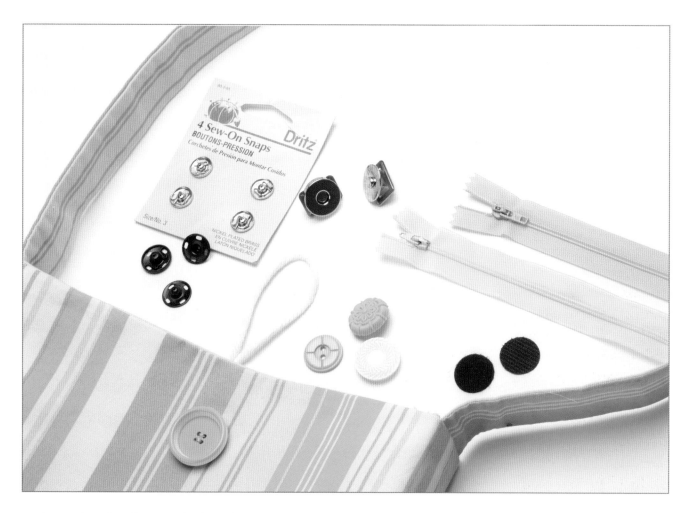

A closure for a handbag can be both functional and decorative. Here are just a few of the many possible fasteners you can use to give your handbag the perfect finishing touch.

CLOTHING SNAPS

Ordinary snaps made for clothing can be used as closures on handbags. Choose large snaps and sew to the inside of the purse with strong thread. Use one large snap in the center or sew several in a row to close the top opening of the bag. Add the snaps to the lining before assembling the purse to hide the backs of the snaps on the inside.

ZIPPERS

To use a zipper for a closure, follow the manufacturer's instructions and baste the zipper into place on the main body fabric panels. Sew the zipper to connect the purse panels before beginning purse construction. Open the zipper as you continue making the finished purse, tacking the lining to the sides of the zipper inside the purse.

19

basic tools

Having the right tools will make handbag construction a breeze. You can avoid a lot of frustration if you have good sewing scissors, cutting and measuring tools, and a few other basic tools. Having the proper tools helps to make your work look more professional. It also allows you to work quickly, especially if you are making multiple pieces.

Various scissors and cutting tools used in these projects. Use the best cutting tool for the material you are using to make the project easier and to protect the tools from unnecessary wear or damage.

SELF-HEALING MATS

Self-healing mats are marked with grids for easy measuring and cutting. Large mats are available in the quilting section of fabric stores. Smaller mats, which are commonly used for setting eyelets and grommets (see below), are available through scrapbook leather suppliers.

CUTTING TOOLS

A sharp pair of sewing scissors will allow you to trim seams close to the stitching and clip corners in tight areas. Rotary cutters, popular with quilters, help you to cut clean lines quickly and with precision.

This type of cutter is especially helpful for square or rectangular designs. Leather shears cut leather with ease. Paper scissors and small cuticle scissors are useful to have on hand for various tasks used in handbag construction.

EYELET SETTER & MALLET

Grommets and eyelets, traditional leather-crafting supplies, can be used to make reinforced holes in handbags. The holes give a place to attach a handle or serve decorative purposes.

A few helpful items for your toolbox: hand drill, metal punch, eyelet setter and mat, wire cutters, and pliers.

They are available in a wide variety of sizes and colors. You can find them in craft, fabric, and scrapbooking stores. To set a grommet or eyelet, you will need a setter and a hammer or mallet. Punch a hole matching the size of the eyelet in the material. Hammer the eyelet into place over an eyelet mat or board made for the type of eyelets you are using to ensure success.

METAL PUNCH

A handheld metal punch will cut right through metal with ease to make a perfectly shaped hole to set an eyelet into or to attach a handle.

PLIERS & WIRE CUTTERS

Pliers and wire cutters are needed when incorporating wire or cable into a design. Standard needle-nose pliers are sufficient for most tasks. Round-nose pliers come in handy if you want to make round loops as part of your design. Wire cutters are available through jewelry suppliers for clipping the ends of the wire neatly. When working with heavy-gauge wire, use an old pair of wire cutters so you don't dull a good pair.

HAND DRILL

A hand drill is a useful tool for drilling through wood, plastic, or heavy cardboard. Fiskars® makes an excellent drill with a hand crank. It will drill through plastic better than an electric drill, which heats up the plastic and melts it to the bit. You can drill holes through plastic charms to embellish a finished handbag.

glues & adhesives

There are glues and adhesives made for every type of material. Each kind of glue or adhesive has specific properties, making one preferable over another for a specific task. Some adhesives are multi-purpose glues and will adhere both porous and non-porous surfaces. Other types of glue are made especially for fabric or plastic and metal. Read the manufacturer's instructions carefully for proper use and safety precautions. Protect your eyes, skin, and respiratory system. Use proper ventilation and work away from food.

BRAND NAMES

Brand names have been mentioned throughout the projects as a guide when looking for supplies, because it can be frustrating trying to figure out which glue or craft supply you need. You may find other brands that work equally well. There is also a resource section for my favorite fabric and craft supplies at the end of the book. Many of the suppliers are very helpful in choosing the right materials to suit the project you are working on.

IRON-ON ADHESIVE is perfect for adding fabric decorations to handbags. It is sold in sheet form or on rolls in strips of varying widths. The adhesive is double-sided and is heat-activated. Iron the adhesive onto the wrong side of the piece of fabric or appliqué you want to attach. Then iron the fabric or appliqué onto the right side of a fabric surface. The heat will bond both surfaces together.

ADHESIVE SHEETS, such as PEELnSTICK™, work without heat and have adhesive on both sides to bond surfaces together. The adhesive works with paper, fabric, and other smooth materials and allows the fabric or paper to adhere evenly for a smooth, finished surface.

FABRIC GLUE adheres fabric pieces together. It also works well for felt, ribbon, and trim. Fabric glue can be used to hold seams permanently or to tack areas in place without pins as you sew.

ALL-PURPOSE WHITE GLUE, like Sobo® craft and fabric glue, is used to attach small fabric elements and paper, or to seal and finish surfaces. It also works to prevent fraying in place of hem sealant. It dries clear and remains flexible. Test a small area of material before using white glue on fabric or trim.

DECOUPAGE GLUE, such as Mod Podge® decoupage glue, seals paper to protect the surface from wear and moisture. It is available in a matte or gloss finish. The glue is thin and can be applied with a brush. Apply several coats, letting each coat dry between layers.

GEM AND JEWEL GLUES

are designed to glue buttons, gems, and charms to porous surfaces like fabric. Two brands of this type of glue are Gem-Tac™ and Aleene's Jewel-It®. Gem glue also works well for attaching trims and cord to fabric. Gem glue needs to dry overnight. Some brands will survive gentle washing, which makes them ideal for fabric.

HEM SEALANT,

such as Fray Check™, dries clear and is used to prevent fraying of fabric or cord. Use this type of glue to secure knots of thread or around slits in fabric to prevent fraying.

GEL-TYPE

adhesives, such as E6000® and FPC9001™, work well on metal, glass, plastic, and other non-porous surfaces. Use this type of glue with good ventilation and away from food preparation areas. These adhesives should be left to dry overnight.

When using adhesives for making handbags, choose the best type for the task at hand, whether you're using it to bond metal or plastic, stop cord from fraying, or protect surfaces.

sewing techniques

A few simple stitches and techniques are used in the construction of some of the bags in this book. If you sew clothes, you may already be familiar with these techniques. They work equally well for making handbags.

TYPES OF STITCHES

Here are a few types of stitches that are used most often for the projects in this book. Practice making new stitches on scraps of fabric before starting to sew a purse.

A BASTING STITCH is a long stitch used to tack pieces together temporarily. You can make a basting stitch either by hand or by using the largest stitch on a sewing machine.

TOPSTITCHING can be functional or decorative. Stitch by machine about ¼ inch from the edge of the finished seam of the fabric. Use the edge of your presser foot as a guide for a nice, even stitching line.

EDGE STITCHING is similar to topstitching, but is done very close to the finished edge of the seam. The stitching line is about ¹⁄₁₆ to ⅛ inch from the edge.

THE BLANKET STITCH, which is also called the buttonhole stitch, is a decorative embroidery stitch. Use embroidery floss or craft thread to stitch around the edge of the fabric to decorate the bag. To make a blanket stitch, pull the floss through the fabric from the back to the front about ¼ inch from the edge. Make a loop of thread and poke the needle into the front of the fabric and out the back a short distance away (about ¼ inch from the edge). Bring the needle straight up through the looped floss, making sure the needle is in front of the loop as shown in the photo at right. Pull the floss gently and repeat to continue stitching around the fabric.

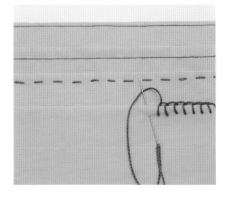

A few basic stitches. From top to bottom: edge stitching, topstitching, basting, and blanket stitch.

USING A ZIPPER FOOT

Using a zipper foot is an obvious choice for stitching a zipper in place, but the foot is also helpful in many other instances. Use a zipper foot when you are trying to sew close to a handbag handle or metal tab. Another use for a zipper foot is applying beaded trim or fringe. The foot will allow you to sew close to the edge of the trim without running over the beads or getting them caught in the machine.

USING STABILIZER

Stabilizer is a handy item to have around. It is sold in small rolls in the notions section of the fabric store. Stabilizer acts as a barrier between the sewing machine and certain types of "hard-to-sew" fabrics, such as oilcloth and leather, and helps the fabric glide along without catching or sticking in the machine. It can be removed after sewing. Different types of stabilizing fabric include dissolvable, tear-away, and cut-away. The tear-away type is used when stabilizer is called for in the projects in this book.

CLIPPING & GRADING SEAMS

Clipping and grading seams reduces bulk when you turn fabric pieces right side out and press. When you grade, you trim layered seams to vary the width of each. Curved seams require clipping to allow the fabric to conform to the curve. Reduce bulk in corners by making clips at inner corners or clip off corners to reduce bulk. This will make crisp, neat corners and contours.

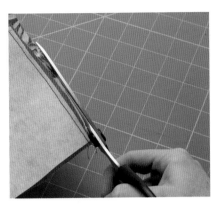

Grading seams. Trim the top layer first, very close to the stitching line (about ⅛ inch from the line). Trim each successive layer a little wider.

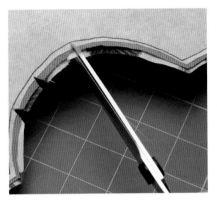

Clip seams around curved areas to allow ease in the curve when the piece is turned right side out.

THREAD

Select thread that is compatible with the type of fabric or material you are using to construct your handbag.

SEWING THREAD is sufficient for most fabrics. Use extra-strong thread or button thread to sew beads, buttons, or cord handles onto a bag.

MONOFILAMENT THREAD is clear like fishing line. Use this type of thread if you don't want it to show.

EMBROIDERY FLOSS, or craft thread from DMC®, is functional and decorative. Heavier decorative threads can be used to stitch together pieces, such as panels for a felt purse. Embroidery stitches are used to create a surface design on the body of a bag or purse. Use interfacing to help stabilize the fabric when using decorative stitching on a bag. If you complete the decorative stitching before assembling the bag, the lining fabric will hide the back side of the stitching.

sew easy
bags

Unlike clothing and home decor projects that require a lot of time and commitment, handbags are quick and simple to make, and a fun way to satisfy your desire to work with your hands. If you are new to sewing, a purse is a great beginner's project.

These bags were made with the following fabrics from Michael Miller Fabrics: Funky Flowers, Flamingo Dots, and Chic Stripe.

classic fabric tote

This simple, but elegant bag requires no pattern and can be made with a variety of fabrics, from cotton novelty prints to upholstery fabrics. You can sew your own strap or choose plastic, wooden, or bamboo handles to coordinate with your design. Try varying the dimensions for a different look. If you sew a button on the lining fabric, you can turn the bag inside out to make it reversible.

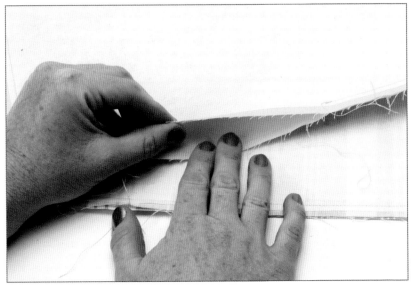

TO MAKE ONE 11- BY 8-INCH BAG, YOU WILL NEED

1 yard fabric for outside of bag

⅓ yard lining fabric

1 yard heavyweight fusible interfacing

12-inch-long cord for closure

Large button for closure

Cardboard or plastic canvas for bottom of bag (optional)

1. Cut two pieces of fabric for the outside of the tote and two for the lining (cut each 12 inches wide by 9 inches high). Cut a strip 3½ inches wide by 36 inches long from the remaining outside fabric for the strap. Cut interfacing for all of the pieces, including the strap, and iron to the wrong side of each piece.

2. Place the outside fabric pieces with right sides together and stitch side and bottom seams, using a ½-inch seam allowance, to form the tote. Place lining pieces with the right sides together and stitch the side seams and part of the bottom seam; leave an opening in the bottom of the lining for turning later.

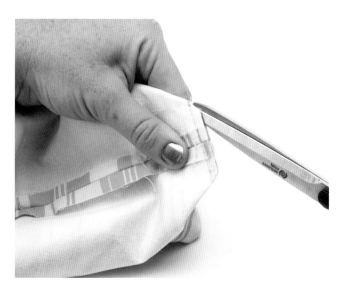

3. To form bottom corners, pinch the fabric at the bottom of one of the corners to make a triangle with the seam in the middle (the side and bottom seams should match). Measure 1 inch from the point and stitch across the seam.

4. Clip off the excess triangle of fabric. Make a small clip on each side to open up the seam. Sew the remaining corners of the tote and the lining pieces in the same fashion. Turn the outside fabric section right side out and press the seams. Leave the lining inside out and press; set the tote aside.

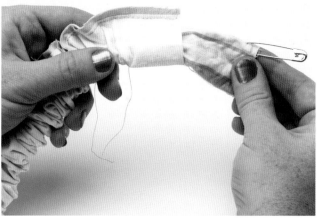

5. Fold the strap piece lengthwise with the right sides together. Stitch along the long edge using a ½-inch seam allowance. Trim the seam.

6. Turn the strap right side out using a large safety pin. Press the finished strap.

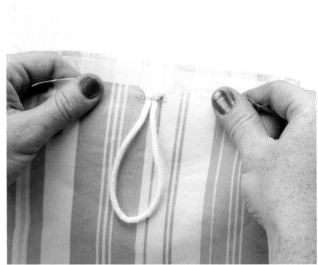

7. Pin the strap to the side seams of the tote on the right side of the tote, matching the ends of the strap to the top edge of the fabric.

8. Pin a loop of cord for the closure at the top center edge of the tote. Adjust the size of the loop as needed to fit the button size and placement on the finished tote. Baste the straps and cord into place.

9. Slip the finished tote section into the lining with the right sides together. Take care to tuck the strap into the bottom of the tote to keep it from getting caught in the seams.

10. Stitch around the top edge through all thicknesses, using a ½-inch seam allowance. Trim the seam to ¼ inch.

11. Turn the bag right side out by pulling the fabric through the opening in the lining. Press the tote.

12. For added support, cut cardboard or plastic canvas to match the dimensions of the bottom of the bag. Slip the piece into the bottom of the tote through the opening in the lining.

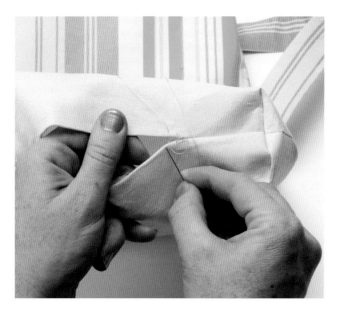

13. Stitch up the opening in the lining by hand.

14. Sew a large button to the front of the bag, adjusting the placement of the button to match up with the cord loop.

VARIATIONS

For a different look, you can make a bag with two straps, or sew tabs to hold purchased handles in place. Sew straps by cutting two fabric strips $2\frac{1}{2}$ inches wide by 23 inches long. Iron interfacing onto the wrong side of the straps, fold each strap in half lengthwise, and stitch with the right sides together using a $\frac{3}{8}$-inch seam allowance. Trim the seams and turn the straps right side out. Baste the straps to the bag $2\frac{1}{2}$ inches from each side.

To make tabs for handles, cut a strip of fabric $2\frac{1}{2}$ inches wide by 12 inches long. Fold the strip in half lengthwise and stitch with right sides together using a $\frac{3}{8}$-inch seam allowance. Trim the seams and turn the sewn strip right side out. Cut the piece into four equal parts. Mark the position of the tabs at the top of the bag using the purchased handles for placement. Fold each tab in half, wrap around handles, and baste to the top edges of the front and back of the tote (finished tabs should measure about 1 inch long). Note: When sewing the bag, be sure to leave the opening in the lining wide enough for the handles to pass through.

To add a decorative trim, sew trim along the top edge of the right side of the fabric for the outside of the bag before assembly. Sew a strip of fabric or ribbon onto the outside fabric of the bag to cover the top edge of the trim.

oilcloth tote

Oilcloth is a colorful, stain-resistant vinyl fabric that cleans up easily with a damp sponge. Oilcloth is typically 47 inches wide, allowing you to make several totes from just 1 yard of fabric. This tote is made from a rectangle, but you can change the dimensions to make a custom tote of any size. Measure beach towels or magazines to make a tote specifically for the items you are carrying.

TO MAKE ONE 11- BY 8-INCH TOTE, YOU WILL NEED

1 yard oilcloth fabric for outside of tote

1 yard coordinating oilcloth fabric for lining

Tear-away stabilizer

Plastic canvas or cardboard for the base

1. Cut two pieces of oilcloth, one for the outside of the tote and one for the lining, each 12 inches wide by 20 inches long. Cut a strip 2 inches wide by 36 inches long for the handles. Fold the piece for the outside in half with the right sides together. The folded piece will measure 12 inches wide by 10 inches tall. Stitch both side seams with a ¼-inch seam allowance. When working with oilcloth, use a long stitch length of about eight stitches per inch. Clip the seams open on both corners, being careful not to cut through the stitching.

2. Use your fingers to press the seams open at the corners. Pinch the fabric at the bottom of one of the corners to make a triangle with the seam in the middle (the side and bottom seams will be matched up). Do this for both corners.

3. Measure 1 inch from the point of each triangle and stitch through the layers of fabric, across the open seam, to form the bottom and side corners of the tote.

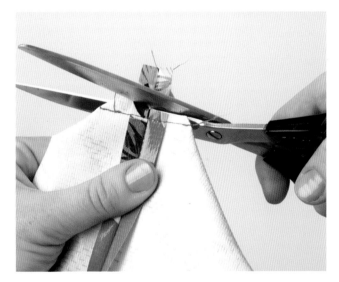

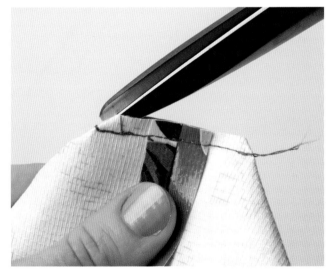

4. Clip off the excess fabric triangles, trimming close to the stitching.

5. Clip the seams open on both sides and turn the piece right side out. Repeat steps 1 through 5 for the lining fabric. Leave the lining turned inside out.

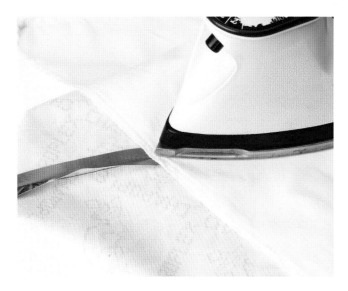

6. Press the seams open using the silk setting on an iron. Use a press cloth to keep the oilcloth from sticking to the iron.

7. To make the handles, cut a long strip of tear-away stabilizer to place under the fabric as you sew. Fold the raw edges on each side into the middle of the strip. The 2-inch wide strip will be folded into thirds to make a handle about ⅝ inch wide. You only need to fold a few inches of the strip to get started; you can continue folding the edges in as you stitch.

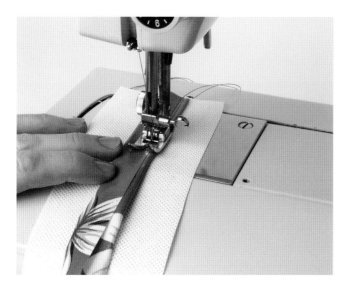

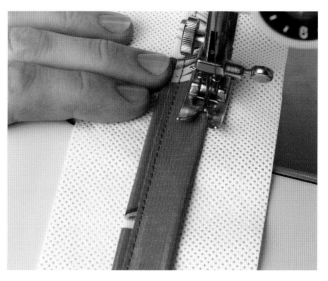

8. Stitch close to the raw edge of the top folded third.

9. Stitch the other side of the handle down the length of the strap. When finished, you will have two neat rows of stitching.

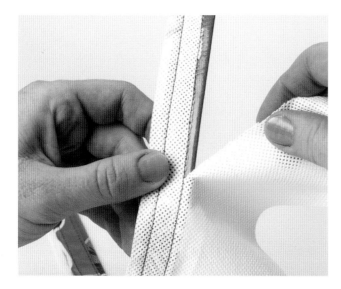

10. Remove the tear-away stabilizer and cut the strip in half to make two handles.

11. Place the handles 2 ½ inches from the side seams on the right side of the outside fabric, matching handle ends to the raw edge of the tote. Baste in place ¼ inch from the raw edge.

12. Place the outside of the bag into the lining. Keep the handles down inside the tote and match top edges and side seams.

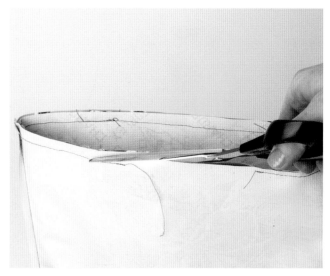

13. Stitch around the top of the bag using a ⅜-inch seam allowance. Leave the space between one of the handles open for turning. Trim the seam to ¼ inch. Turn the fabric right side out, pulling the fabric through the opening left at the top. Press using a press cloth.

14. To make a support for the base of the bag, cut a rectangle slightly smaller than the base of the bag (about 9 inches by 1¾ inch) from plastic canvas material. Slip this through the opening to the bottom of the bag between the lining and outside layers.

15. Topstitch close to the edge around the top of the tote. This will close the opening as well as give the tote a finished look.

HINTS FOR WORKING WITH OILCLOTH

Oilcloth is a sturdy material that is ideal for making durable and stylish totes, but there are a few things to keep in mind when working with this fabric.

- Do not use pins as they will tear the cloth.
- Use a press cloth to protect the vinyl from direct heat when ironing.
- Use tear-away stabilizer as you sew on the right side (smooth vinyl side) of the oilcloth. This will keep it from sticking to the machine and feed dogs as you sew.
- Oilcloth does not fray, so finished seams are not necessary.
- Use your pressure foot as a seam guide to sew narrow seams. This will allow you to sew the bag quickly without having to trim the seams.
- Use a longer stitch to avoid weakening the fabric.

ADD A BORDER

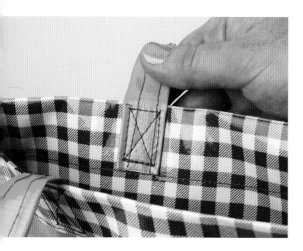

To add a contrasting border of fabric at the top of the bag, cut the lining fabric 2½ inches longer than the fabric for the outside. This will cause the finished lining to extend above the top of the bag. Sew both the outside and lining as described in the standard tote pattern following steps 1 through 6. Place the lining inside the outside piece and fold the extending edge of the lining over to make a border around the top of the bag. Topstitch very close to the raw edge of the lining on the outside of the tote. Place the handles on the inside of the tote. Handles should be placed as they will be on the finished bag, as they will not be turned up. Stitch the handles to the sides of the bag with the bottom of the handle strips aligned with the top-stitching. Stitch a rectangle with an **X** in the middle to hold the handle strips securely to the sides.

TRAPEZOID PURSE

Cut two pieces of oilcloth 12 inches wide by 16 inches long—one for the outside and one for the lining. Fold one of the pieces in half (right sides together) to measure 12 inches wide by 8 inches high. Measure 2 inches from each side at the top and mark. Draw a diagonal line down to the bottom corners. You will have a trapezoid shape measuring 8 inches wide at the top and 12 inches wide at the bottom. Stitch along these lines. Trim off the excess close to the stitching. Form the bottom and side corners as described for the standard tote (steps 2–5), except measure ⅝ inch from the point of the triangle. Repeat the same steps for the lining piece. Follow the directions for finishing the purse as described for the standard tote, making a single strap out of a piece of oilcloth cut 1½ inches wide by 38 inches long. Attach the strap to the side seams of the purse before stitching and turning.

hoop handle
bag

Round handles made of bamboo or plastic convert simple upholstery bags into fashion statements. The project instructions are for a large bag with round, 7-inch bamboo handles. To make a smaller bag, cut fabric pieces 14 inches wide by 12 inches high and use round, 5-inch handles. Whichever size you choose to make, heavyweight interfacing will help the bag to stand up firmly. When choosing fabric for the lining, keep in mind that this bag can be reversible.

TO MAKE ONE 15- BY 12-INCH BAG, YOU WILL NEED

½ yard fabric for outside of bag

½ yard lining fabric

½ yard heavyweight fusible interfacing

Round 7-inch bamboo hoop handles (Bag Boutique™ by Prym Dritz)

Cardboard or plastic canvas for bottom of bag (optional)

1. Cut two pieces of fabric for the outside of the purse and two pieces for the lining; each piece should measure 16 inches wide by 14 inches high. To make handle tabs, cut two 3- by 18-inch strips from the remaining outside fabric. Cut interfacing for the outside and lining pieces and fuse with an iron to the wrong side of each piece. The tab pieces do not need interfacing. Trace or copy the larger pattern on page 45. Place the pattern at the center of the 16-inch side of the outside fabric pieces and trace around the shape on the right side of the fabric. This line will be your stitching line.

2. Cut a half circle ½ inch inside the stitching line out of each panel of outside fabric.

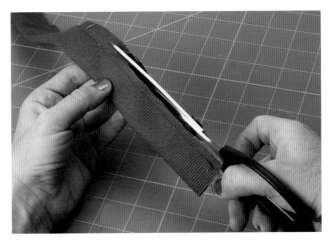

3. To make the handle tabs, fold the tab strips in half lengthwise with right sides together. Sew a seam using a ½-inch allowance. Trim close to stitching. Use a safety pin to turn the strips right side out. Press the strips. Cut each strip into three equal pieces to make six pieces in total.

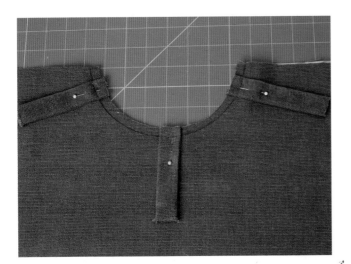

4. For each handle, position three tabs around the curve on the right side of the outside fabric; place one tab in the center of the curve and a tab on each side $\frac{5}{8}$ inch from the top edge of the fabric. Pin the tabs in place and baste along the stitching line.

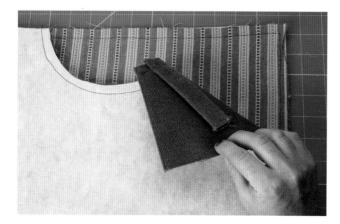

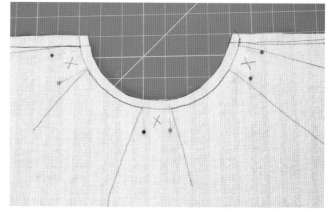

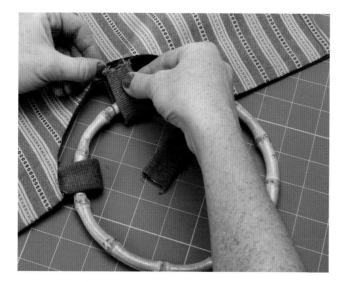

5. Place the fabric with tabs basted in place onto the corresponding lining piece with right sides together.

6. Pin all of the layers together along the top and around the curve, placing pins on each side of the tabs. Cut the lining to match the cut curve of the front piece. Stitch the lining to the front piece, sewing along the basting line. Do not stitch over the tabs, as you will need to leave an opening at each tab. The pins will help avoid accidentally sewing over a tab. Sew the seam with a ½-inch seam allowance.

Trim the seam to ¼ inch and clip off corners. Clip along the curve, being careful not to cut through stitching (see "Clipping & Grading Seams" on page 25). Turn the pieces right side out and press.

7. Position the hoop handle, wrapping each tab over the handle. Slip each tab into each opening in the fabric along the curve. Reach between the fabric and lining to cinch up each tab over the handle. Pin the tabs in place.

8. Use a zipper foot to stitch around the curve on the right side of the fabric, stitching close to the pressed edge and through all thicknesses and stitching over all three tabs. Finish the other side of the purse following steps 4 through 8.

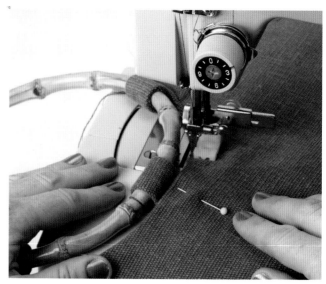

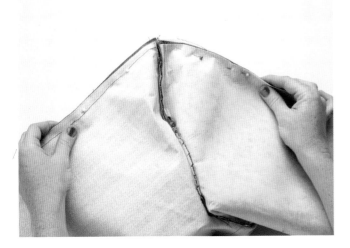

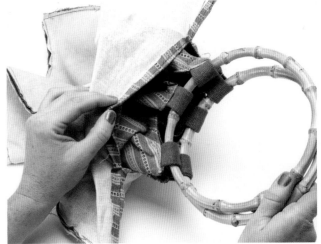

9. Open up each finished piece and pin the two together with right sides facing. Stitch around the entire piece with a ½-inch seam allowance, leaving an opening along the bottom edge of the lining to allow the handles to pass through. Stitch slowly, adjusting the fabric as you work to keep the seams even and the fabric from shifting. To form corners at the bottom of the bag, follow steps 3 and 4 of the classic fabric tote on page 30, sewing across the corners 1¼ inches from the points of the triangles. Trim the seams.

10. Turn bag right side out, pulling the handles through the opening of the lining. Press the bag. For extra support, cut cardboard or plastic canvas to match the dimensions of the bottom of the bag and slip into the opening in the lining. Stitch up the opening in the lining by hand to finish the bag.

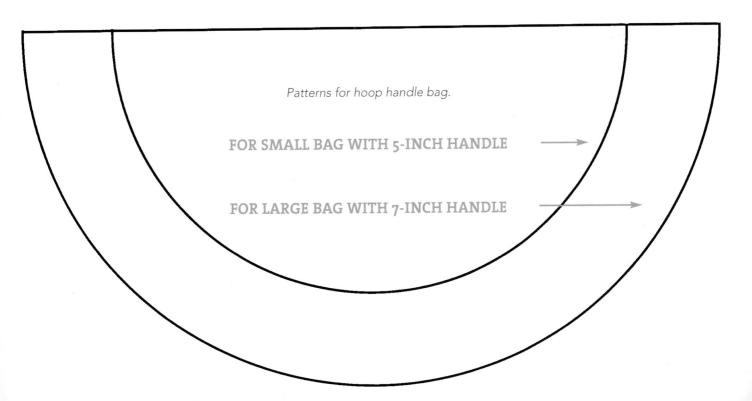

Patterns for hoop handle bag.

FOR SMALL BAG WITH 5-INCH HANDLE →

FOR LARGE BAG WITH 7-INCH HANDLE →

woven ribbon
purse

This project is a great way to use up lots of ribbon scraps. You can combine ribbon with other materials, such as bias tape, jute, and lace. Just make sure they'll all hold up to heat so they won't melt from the heat of the iron.

1. Lay the fusible interfacing face up on the cardboard. Cut ribbons into strips long enough to cover the length of the interfacing (approximately 18 inches long in this case), then arrange them edge-to-edge so that its entire width is covered. Pin ribbons along the top edge of the interfacing, making sure to angle the pins away from the ribbons so that they won't interfere with ironing in step 3.

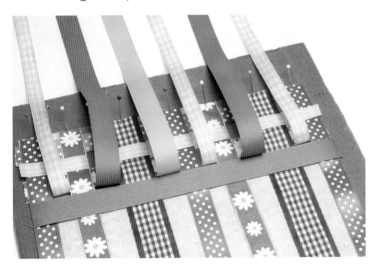

TO MAKE ONE 11- BY 7-INCH PURSE, YOU WILL NEED

14- by 18-inch piece of heavyweight fusible interfacing

Corrugated cardboard (at least 14 by 18 inches)

Pins

Ribbon:

　1 yard $^5/_8$-inch yellow grosgrain

　2 yards $1^1/_2$-inch orange and pink plaid

　2 yards $^7/_8$-inch pink and white polka dot

　2 yards $^5/_8$-inch yellow gingham check

　2$^1/_2$ yards $^7/_8$-inch orange/daisy print

　5 yards $^7/_8$-inch pink grosgrain (3 yards for purse; 2 yards for handles)

12- by 16-inch piece of cotton fabric in a coordinating color or print (for lining)

1 yard $1^1/_2$-inch rickrack

Metal purse handle loops

2. Cut another set of ribbons the length of the width of the interfacing; cut enough to cover the entire length of the interfacing. To weave the shorter pieces into the pinned ribbon, lift up every other vertical ribbon and slide the horizontal ribbon in place; on the next row lift the alternate ribbons up before adding the next ribbon. Alternate the over-under pattern until all of the interfacing is covered.

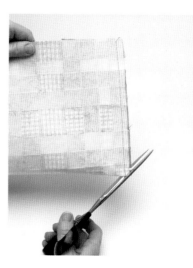

3. Iron the ribbons to the interfacing on a low to medium setting; cover the ribbons with a press cloth while ironing to prevent them from sticking or melting.

4. To make the body of the purse, trim the ribbon "fabric" to 12 inches by 16 inches, then fold it in half, right sides together, to make a rectangle 12 inches wide by 8 inches tall. Stitch the side seams using a ⅜-inch seam allowance. Clip the seam open on both corners, being careful not to cut through the stitching.

5. To form corners at the bottom of the bag, follow steps 3 and 4 of the classic fabric tote on page 30, sewing across the corners ⅝ inch from the points of the triangles. Turn the purse right side out. Make the lining for the purse by following steps 4 and 5, but do not turn the lining inside out. Press the purse body and the seams on the lining using a low to medium setting on the iron. Use a press cloth to keep the ribbons from sticking to the iron.

6. Use small pieces of ribbon to attach the metal handle hardware. Pin the rickrack and the ribbon loops to the top edge of the right side of the purse body.

7. Baste around the top of the purse, stitching down the center of the rickrack and across the ribbon loops. Slip the body of the purse into the lining, right sides together, matching side seams and top edges.

8. Pin and sew around the top through all layers, stitching along the rickrack. Leave an opening between the handle loops on one side for turning. Trim the seam to ¼ inch, grading it to reduce bulk (see page 25).

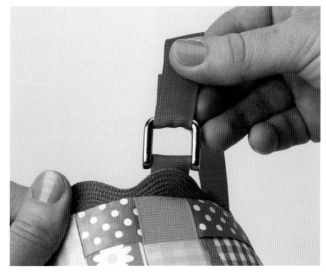

9. Turn the purse right side out through the opening at the top. Push the lining inside and press the seams using a press cloth. Hand stitch the top opening closed.

10. For each handle, thread an 18-inch length of ribbon through the metal hardware on each side of the purse and stitch across it to secure.

crocheted
purse

For this project, strips of fabric are crocheted together. The pattern of the fabric will not show in the stitching, so choose fabrics according to color, not pattern. This project is a great way to use up all of the novelty prints you've saved and never had a use for. Cotton fabrics tear into strips easily to make the "yarn" to crochet. This purse can also be knitted, instead of crocheted, if you prefer.

TO MAKE ONE 10- BY 8-INCH PURSE, YOU WILL NEED

2 yards cotton print fabric to crochet

½ yard fabric for lining and flower decoration

Large crochet hook (size P)

Small bamboo purse handles

1. Tear the fabric with the grain into ¾-inch strips. Join the strips by cutting a slit in the end of each strip of fabric. Slip the end of one of the strips (this will be strip #1) through the slit of the other (strip #2).

2. Pull the "tail" of strip #1 back through its own slit.

3. Pull the strips gently until they are tight. Roll the joined strips into a ball and add additional strips as needed.

4. To begin crocheting, start with a slip knot: First, make a loop, leaving a short tail of fabric.

5. Pull the working end of the strip through the loop with the crochet hook.

6. Adjust the tension, so that the loop isn't too tight or too loose on the hook.

7. To begin the first stitch, wrap the strip around the crochet hook.

8. Pull the fabric through the loop. This is one chain stitch. Chain stitch sixteen more times to begin the bottom of the purse.

9. To begin the first row, hook into the third chain from the hook. Wrap the fabric strip around the hook and pull the loop of fabric through the chain stitch.

10. Wrap the strip around the hook again and pull through two loops on the hook this time to finish the stitch. This completes one single crochet stitch. Continue down the chain, creating one single crochet in each chain.

11. When you reach the last stitch, single crochet twice in the same stitch to round the corner at the end of the row. (This photo shows two completed single crochet stitches in the same chain stitch at the end of the row.)

sew easy bags

12. Continue to single crochet around the back side of the chain. When you reach the end of the row, single crochet the same stitch twice. This completes one row.

13. Single crochet until you reach the end of the row and stitch twice in one of the stitches at the end of the row in the middle of the curve. Continue down the row and finish the row with two stitches in one of the stitches at the end (in the center of the curve). This completes the second row. There should be a total of thirty-four stitches around the row. To form the sides of the purse, continue to single crochet around the rows. Build the sides of the purse with rows of stitches until you have completed fourteen rows in total (or until you are pleased with the height of the bag). Finish with a slip stitch by hooking the end of the fabric strip through the last stitch and pulling the end of the strip to tighten. Weave the end tail of the fabric strip into the work to hide.

14. To attach handles, cut a piece of fabric 9 inches wide by 5 inches tall. Fold the piece in half to measure 4½ inches with right sides together and stitch a ½-inch seam on the open 5-inch side. Turn right side out and press. Loop the fabric over the handle and stitch along the bottom edge. Stitch the handle tab inside the bag by hand. Repeat for the other side.

15. To make the lining, measure the finished bag and cut fabric the width of the bag and twice the height. Stitch both sides with the right sides together using a narrow seam. Fold the raw edge of the lining over about ½ inch and press. Slip the lining into the bag and hand stitch around the top inside the bag.

FABRIC FLOWER

You can dress up this simple bag by making three-dimensional embellishments out of extra scraps of fabric. Bows, flowers, and fringe are just a few examples of how you can express your creativity to create something really special. For this fabric flower, iron-on adhesive is applied between layers to help the petals stand up and hold their shape.

1. Fuse together two layers of fabric (8- by 8-inch piece or small scraps) by ironing HeatnBond® Lite Iron-on Adhesive onto the wrong side of one piece of fabric, removing the protective paper, and ironing the other layer of fabric to the back (wrong sides together).

2. Trace around three or four drinking glasses of various sizes on the fabric to make concentric circles for the layers of the flower.

3. Cut out the circles and make small clips around the edges to make "petals." Curl the petals with your fingers to add dimension. Layer the circles starting with the biggest and ending with the smallest. Glue in between each layer with fabric glue.

4. Glue the flower to the finished bag with fabric or gem glue. Glue a button in the middle with gem glue. Let the glue dry.

PLASTIC BAG PURSE

For a interesting twist, try making this purse with plastic bags instead of fabric. You will need either twenty-five to thirty small plastic grocery bags or ten large trash bags to make one purse.

1. Smooth and flatten the bags and cut into strips about 1 inch wide across the width of the bags to make loops. You can stack up to five bags together and cut all at once. Because the bag strips are already loops, you will not need to cut slits in them to link together. Insert the end of one loop into the opening of another.

2. Pull the tail of the first strip through its own loop. Pull the strips gently to tighten or they may tear. Crochet the plastic "yarn" as directed for the fabric bag.

Make a strap for the bag by attaching a plastic bag loop to the top of the bag on one side and chain stitch until you are pleased with the length. Hook into the opposite side with a slip stitch and single crochet back along the chain until you reach the starting point of the strap. Tie off the end and weave the tail of the loop into the work to hide.

patchwork photo
transfer bag

Any image or photo can be transferred onto fabric using an ink jet printer. Paper-backed fabric sheets are sold especially for this purpose. Combining printed images with fabrics, vintage lace, trims, and buttons creates a keepsake reminiscent of an heirloom quilt.

TO MAKE ONE 10- BY 7-INCH BAG, YOU WILL NEED

Collage sheet (Aspen Art Stamps)

Cotton poplin ink jet fabric sheet (The Vintage Workshop)

⅓ yard fusible fleece (cut two pieces 12 by 9 inches each)

½ yard medium- or heavyweight fusible interfacing (cut two 12- by 9-inch pieces for lining and two 2- by 24-inch strips for straps)

Six different fabrics (fat quarters or scraps)

Buttons, large beads, and brass embellishments

½ yard fabric for lining and straps

Large button and cord for closure

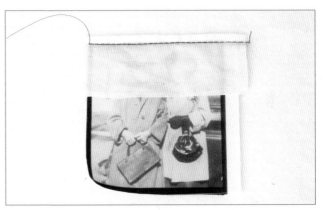

1. Follow manufacturer's instructions to print collage images onto fabric sheet using an ink jet printer. The fabric sheet has full instructions for transferring images, including the scanning instructions. Peel the paper backing off the printed fabric. Cut out the fabric image to use for the center design of the quilt, leaving a ¼-inch border around the image for the seam allowance.

2. Place the cut fabric image in the center of a 12- by 9-inch piece of fusible fleece (piece is horizontal with the fusible side up). Optional: You can back the fleece with fusible interfacing (fusible side up) for stability; the fleece will be sandwiched between the interfacing and the fabric images. Choose one of the fabrics to start with and cut a strip approximately 1¼ inch wide and long enough to cover the top edge of the fabric image. Place the strip on top of the image with the right sides together and stitch through the fabrics, fleece, and interfacing using a ¼-inch-wide seam allowance. Press the seam open with your fingers, right sides out.

3. Add the next strip of fabric to the side of the existing pieces, making sure the strip is long enough to cover both edges. Stitch and press open with fingers. Continue adding strips around each edge, making each strip long enough to cover the existing fabric edges. Vary the widths of the strips, between 1 and 2 inches to make the design more interesting.

4. Sew strips of lace over a few of the finished seams on the right side of the fabric before adding the next strip of fabric. Make sure the lace is long enough to cover the length of the seam.

5. Continue adding fabric pieces around each side. Add a large piece of fabric to each side of the quilting to cover the remaining fleece. Press the quilting on the right and back side of the fabric to fuse the interfacing to the fleece. Follow steps 2 through 6 to make the back of the bag. Trim the front and back panels to 8 by 11 inches. Sew on embellishments to decorate.

6. Cut 1-inch squares from the bottom corners of both the front and back panels.

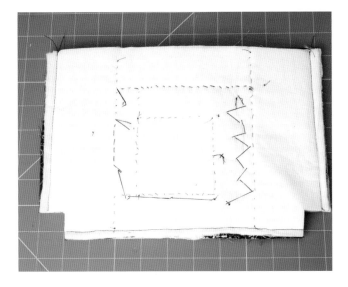

7. Join the front and back panels, right sides together, and stitch the side seams and bottom seam using a ½-inch seam allowance. Trim the seams to ¼ inch.

8. Cut a 15- by 11-inch piece of fabric for the lining. Place right sides together and stitch the sides using a ½-inch seam allowance. Trim the side seams to ¼ inch. Using the finished quilted piece as a guide, cut the corners of the lining to match the measurements of the quilted piece.

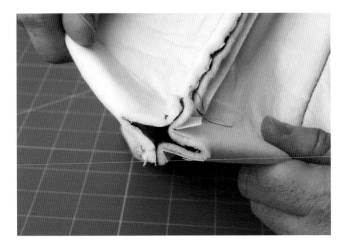

9. To form the sides and corners of the bag, start with one of the corners of the quilted piece and pinch it to match the bottom and side seams. Stitch across the opening with a ¼-inch seam to form the corner.

10. Repeat the process to form the corners of the lining. Press the seams of both the quilted piece and the lining of the bag. Turn the quilted piece right side out; leave the lining inside out.

11. To make the handles of the bag, cut and piece fabric strips together to make two 2- by 34-inch strips. Cut two pieces of interfacing 1¾ inches wide by 34 inches long. Iron the interfacing to the wrong side of the strips.

12. Fold one of the fabric strips lengthwise with the right sides together. Stitch across one end and down the length of the strip using a ⅜-inch seam allowance. Clip the corner and trim the seam to ¼ inch.

13. Turn the sewn strip right side out, using a chopstick or craft stick at the stitched end to aid in turning. Push it down into the strip, sliding the fabric along as you turn it.

14. Press the straps and topstitch close to the edge on both sides of the handles for a neat finish.

15. Pin a loop of cording for the closure to the right side of the back piece. Adjust the cord to fit the placement of a large button on the front. Cut off any excess cord.

16. Pin the handles on both sides as shown, about 2½ inches from the side seams. Baste the handles and cord into place about ⅜ inch from the edge.

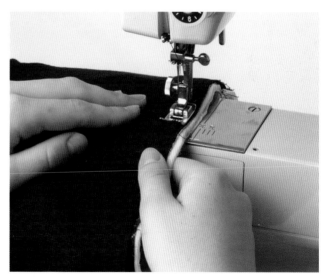

17. Fit the quilted bag into the lining with the right sides together, matching side seams. Be sure to tuck the handles inside. Pin in place.

18. Stitch around the top of the bag using a ½-inch seam allowance. Leave an opening between the handles on one side for turning. Trim the seams to remove bulk and turn the bag right side out. Press the bag and stitch the opening shut. Add a large button to the front for the closure, stitching through all layers of fabric on the front for strength.

glam evening
bag

This bag is the one to use for a formal night out. Sequins and beads add sparkle and highlight the floral pattern on this long sleek purse. Add a beaded handle to complement the design of the bag. You can add other small embellishments, such as brass stampings, larger beads, rhinestones, game pieces, or other dimensional collage elements. Use your bag as a canvas to make a fabulous work of art.

TO MAKE ONE 12- BY 5-INCH BAG, YOU WILL NEED

⅓ yard floral fabric

⅓ yard lining fabric

⅓ yard heavyweight fusible interfacing

9-inch zipper

Heavy plastic-coated wire (14–18 gauge)

Eight 10mm black faceted beads

Sequins, seed beads, and bugle beads for decoration

Clear monofilament thread

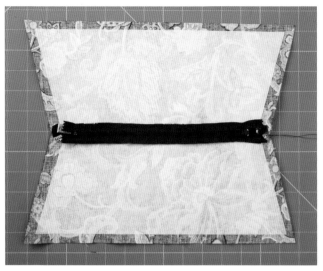

1. Cut two pieces of the floral fabric, lining fabric, and interfacing, each 14 inches wide by 6 inches high. On each piece, mark 1 ½ inches from each side at the top corner and use a straight edge to draw a line from the bottom corner to the mark to make a trapezoid shape. Cut two 2-by 3-inch pieces of fabric for the side tabs.

2. Iron interfacing to the wrong side of the floral fabric pieces. Place the fabric pieces with right sides together. Baste both pieces together along the top edge of the fabric using a ½-inch seam allowance. Press the seam open. Position the right side of the zipper over the basted seam on the wrong side of the fabric. Use a zipper foot to baste the zipper into place following the zipper manufacturer's instructions.

3. Stitch around the zipper on the right side of the fabric, turning corners and stitching above and below the zipper.

4. Make a clip in the seams at both ends of the zipper above the stitching.

5. Use a seam ripper to remove the basting stitches and open the zipper.

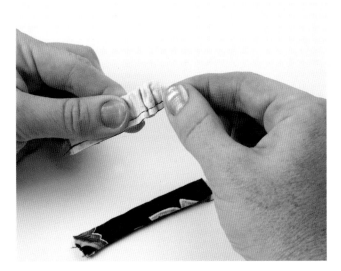

6. To make the tabs, fold the fabric pieces lengthwise and stitch the seams along the 3-inch side with a ⅜-inch seam allowance. Trim close to the stitching and turn right side out with a safety pin. Press the finished tabs.

7. Fold each finished tab in half to make a loop and pin one loop to each side of the bag about ¾ inch down from the top edge, sandwiching it between the front and back fabric pieces. Match the ends of the tab with the edge of the fabric; the loop should face toward the inside of the bag.

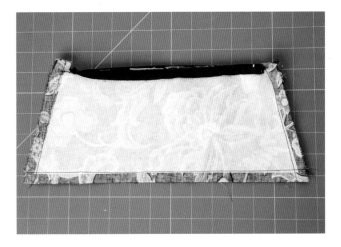

8. Stitch around the sides and bottom of the bag, stitching the tabs into the side seams. Trim the seams to ¼ inch and clip the corners.

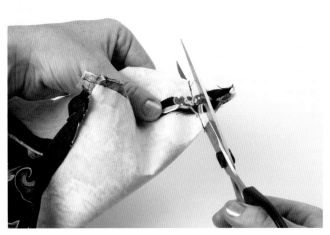

9. To form corners of fabric, pull the fabric at each bottom corner to form a triangle with the seam in the middle, matching the side and bottom seams. Measure 1 inch from the point and stitch across the seam. Clip off the excess triangle of fabric. Turn the bag right side out through the open zipper. Press the seams.

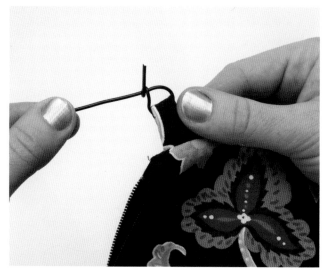

10. Make the lining following steps 8 and 9. Leave the lining inside out and press the seams. Fold the top edge over ½ inch toward the wrong side and press. Set the lining aside and sew into place after step 13.

11. Attach wire through the loop on the side of the bag, twisting it a few times to secure.

12. Add faceted beads to make a handle. Attach the other end of the wire through the loop on the other side and finish by twisting to secure. Clip off excess wire.

13. Sew sequins and beads in place, using a doubled strand of clear monofilament thread. Thread a sequin onto the thread, followed by a seed bead, then bring the needle back through the sequin. The bead will act as a stop bead to anchor the sequin in place. Sew bugle beads and seed beads onto the fabric to add interest, following the color and design of the fabric. You can also use jewel or gem glue to attach sequins and beads.

funky felted
purse

This project is a great way to recycle old, worn-out sweaters. Felting is achieved by washing wool in hot water, rinsing it in cold, and then drying it in a hot dryer. The agitation and the changes in temperature shock and curl the fibers together into a tight weave that will not unravel. Take advantage of stripes and patterns in sweaters to add interest to your design.

TO MAKE ONE 10- BY 7 ½-INCH PURSE, YOU WILL NEED

Large old wool sweater (must be 100-percent wool)

Wool felt scraps for decoration

Embroidery floss

Glass beads for decoration

⅓ yard lining fabric

⅓ yard heavyweight fusible interfacing

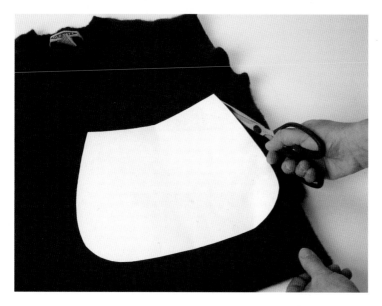

1. Wash the sweater in a washing machine with a small amount of detergent (you can add ¼ cup baking soda to facilitate the felting). Use hot water to wash and cold water to rinse. Place the sweater in a hot dryer to complete the felting. Repeat the process for a tighter weave. (Hint: Place the sweater in a mesh garment bag before washing and drying to reduce the amount of fibers that get caught in the pump of the machine.)

2. Cut two pieces from the sweater using the purse pattern on page 71.

3. Cut out leaf shapes from wool felt, using the patterns on page 71, to decorate the purse.

4. Use a blanket stitch (see page 24) to sew the leaf appliqués onto the front of the purse and then sew the sides of the purse together. Stitch on a few glass beads to decorate.

5. To make the strap of the bag, cut a long 3-inch-wide strip from the felted sweater. Fold in half lengthwise and sew along the long edge with a narrow seam. Trim the seam and turn right side out. Stitch the ends of the strap to the inside of the purse.

6. To make a lining for the bag, cut two pieces each of lining fabric and interfacing using the purse pattern. Iron the interfacing to the wrong side of the lining pieces. Stitch the sides, right sides together, with a narrow ⅜-inch seam. Trim the seams and clip the round corners. Press the top edge over about ½ inch to the wrong side.

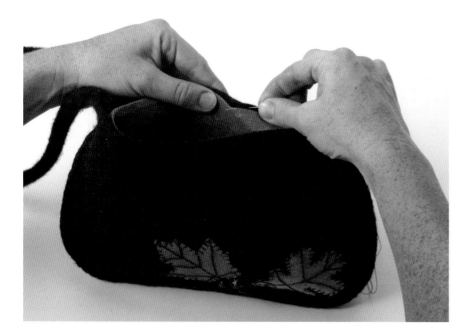

7. Place the lining inside the felted purse and hand stitch the lining to the top inside edge of the purse.

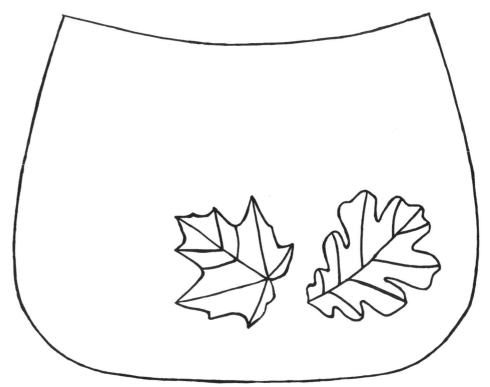

Funky felted purse patterns for front/back panels and appliqués. Enlarge pattern 200 percent.

sew easy bags

multi-colored
woven bag

Inspired by summer crafts projects, this bag you weave on a cardboard loom is a fun way to use up scraps of fabric, ribbon, and yarn. Try combining strips of cotton, denim, or wool with yarn and other fibers to make a highly textured pattern. You can vary the size of the handbag by using a larger piece of cardboard for the loom, or embellish the finished bag with small beads or a large bead closure, if desired.

TO MAKE ONE 7- BY 6-INCH BAG, YOU WILL NEED

Corrugated cardboard (8 inches wide by 7 inches high)

Assorted yarn, fabric scraps, and decorative fibers

Large plastic yarn needle

1. Cut the fibers into varying lengths, leaving most long enough to wrap around the loom a couple of times. Smaller pieces can be used to add texture and spots of color. Join the fibers by tying them together, joining about four or five at a time and adding more as you need them. Start the weaving with several yards of yarn or fabric in a single color. Mark and cut slits across the top of the cardboard ½ inch apart and ½ inch long. You will have fifteen slits when you're finished. Cut one slit in the lower right corner—¼ inch from the right side and about ½ inch long. To start weaving the "warp" yarn, slip the end of the yarn in the first slit on the upper left, leaving a tail about 6 inches long on the front.

73

2. Wrap the yarn around the back of the cardboard loom, around to the front, and back through the first slit at the top.

3. Pull the yarn sideways across the back and through the next slit to the front. Wrap the yarn around the front of the loom, around the back, and through the second slit.

4. Pull the yarn across the front and through to the next slit.

5. Continue wrapping yarn as you did in steps 2 through 5, alternating front to back as you go.

6. Finish by pulling the end through the slit cut at the bottom right of the cardboard. You will have fifteen strips at the front of the loom and sixteen at the back.

7. Start the weaving by tying a "weft" fiber to the end of the warp yarn. Start weaving over and under the warp yarns with the weft fiber.

8. When you reach the end of the first row on the front side, flip the loom over and keep weaving around the back side of the loom. Push the woven strips down with your fingernails as you go to keep the weaving tight. Continue weaving around the loom, adding fiber or fabric strips until you reach the top of the loom.

9. Weave back to the yarn tail at the first slit (where you began in step 1). Tie the ends together to secure. Lift the loops off the slits at the top of the loom and slide the cardboard loom out of the woven purse. Weave the loose ends into the inside of the purse to hide. Make a strap by braiding strips of fabric and tying the ends to the purse to attach.

elegant leather
purse

You can successfully sew leather with an ordinary sewing machine by following a few simple tips. Always use a new sharp needle or a needle made for sewing leather. A non-stick presser foot is recommended for sewing leather, but if you don't have one, sandwiching the leather between strips of tear-away backing works equally well. Both methods will prevent the leather from catching in the machine. Make sure the leather is lightweight and that your machine will handle heavy-duty fabrics.

**TO MAKE ONE 10- BY 8-INCH BAG,
YOU WILL NEED**

Wooden purse handles
  (Bag Boutique)

Gesso

Acrylic paint

Water-based varnish

14- by 21-inch piece of garment-weight
  leather (The Leather Factory)

Tear-away stabilizer

3/4 yard lining fabric (14 inches wide
  by 21 inches long)

Leather glue

Glover's needle

Strong thread

1. Paint the handles with a base coat of gesso and then a coat of acrylic paint to match or contrast the leather. Seal the handles with a coat of varnish after the paint is dry and let the varnish dry overnight.

2. Fold the leather in half with right sides together to form the body of the bag. The folded piece will measure 14 inches wide by 10½ inches tall. Measure 6 inches from the bottom corner along the side seams. Using tear-away stabilizer or a non-stick presser foot, stitch the seams 6 inches in length with a ⅜-inch seam allowance. Leave the rest of the side seams open. Press the seams open, including the unsewn sections. Use a press cloth to protect the leather while pressing. Make a clip through the seams at the point where the stitching stops (6 inches from the bottom).

3. To form the bottom corners of the bag, pull the leather at the bottom corner to form a triangle with the seam in the middle. Measure 1½ inches from the point and stitch across the seam, using tear-away stabilizer as you sew. Remove stabilizer and clip off the triangle of excess leather. Turn the bag right side out.

4. Make the fabric lining for the bag following steps 2 and 3, but leaving the lining inside out. It is not necessary to use tear-away stabilizer on the fabric. Press the seams open.

5. Trim away 1¼ inches of fabric from the top edge of the lining section, then trim away the seam allowances of the open, unstitched portion of the side seams of the lining.

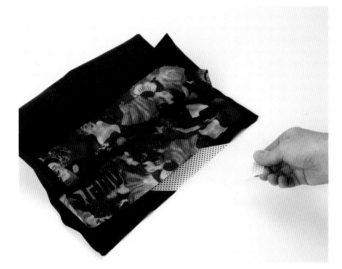

6. Place the lining fabric inside the leather bag with the wrong sides together. Cut a piece of plastic canvas to fit the dimensions of the bottom of the bag and slip the canvas in between the lining and bag to support the bottom.

7. The lining should be positioned inside the bag so that the side seams match up with the leather seams. The clipped seam on the bag marks the point where the stitching ends; match this point to the corresponding stitching on the lining. Align the edge of the lining, which was cut away in step 5, with the pressed crease of the open leather seam, wrong sides together.

8. Use a bead of glue to tack the edge of the lining to the inside open edges of the bag.

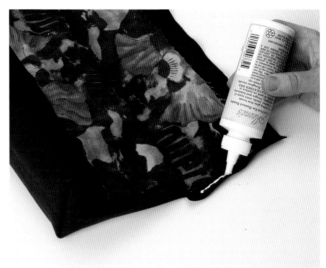

9. Glue the open leather seam over the raw edge of the previously glued lining and press the seam into place. Run a bead of glue under the top edge of the lining to tack the lining to the inside of the bag.

10. Pull approximately 1¾ inches of the leather over the handle to attach. Attach the other handle in the same way, making sure both sides of the bag are even.

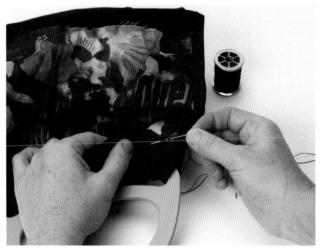

11. Use a glover's needle (sharp needle made especially for hand sewing leather) to stitch the top edge of the leather over the handle to the lining inside the bag. Use a strong thread such as button thread.

SCULPTED LEATHER ROSE

One exciting feature of leather is that it can be shaped and sculpted to make dimensional forms. Realistic-looking leather flowers can be used to embellish an otherwise ordinary leather handbag.

TO MAKE ONE LEATHER ROSE, YOU WILL NEED

Purchased fabric rose

1 square foot or scraps of 2- to 3-ounce vegetable-tanned goat skin (The Leather Factory)

Leather shears

Leather punch (¹/₈-inch hole size or smaller)

Rawhide or plastic mallet

Punch board (The Leather Factory)

Round wooden bead

12-inch piece of wire

Blow dryer

Leather or fabric glue

1. Separate the petals from a fabric flower. If the flower has a large number of petals, you can remove a few. Four petals were used for this leather flower. Trace around the petals on the wrong side of the leather and cut out using leather shears.

LEATHER

Leather is a versatile material. It can be stamped, dyed, painted, or tooled. Leather is very durable, making it great for everyday wear. Leather shops often sell small inexpensive pieces of leather that are the perfect size for making handbags.

It's helpful to have a few specialized tools when working with leather. Leather shears are very sharp and cut leather easily. Leather punches are necessary for making holes in leather. One type is a steel punch that you place over the leather while you strike it with a mallet. The other type is a handheld rotary punch with a wheel that holds various sizes of punches. Other helpful supplies for leather projects include sets for making snaps, eyelets (small metal rings used to reinforce holes in the leather), and leather lace or cord.

2. Punch a small hole in the center of each petal using a leather hole punch and the punch board.

3. Thread the wire through the wooden bead and twist the ends together a few times to secure.

4. Dampen the petals by dipping them in water. Blot each petal with a towel to remove excess water.

5. To build the flower, start with the smallest petal. With the right side of the leather up, curl the top and mold the petals in a cupped shape with your fingers to begin shaping the leather to imitate a natural flower petal.

sew easy bags

6. Apply a small amount of glue close to the center of the petal on the right side of the leather. Slide the petal over the wire, gluing the right side of the petal to the bead.

7. Continue molding the leather and pressing the petals around the center bead.

8. Use a blow dryer to set the leather and dry the shape.

9. Continue adding petals from smallest to largest. Glue between the layers as you add each petal.

10. Mold and shape the petals as you add them, overlapping the petals and holding them with your fingers to form. Blow dry each petal as you add it.

11. Finish the flower by drying the leather with a blow dryer. Bend the wire over on the back side of the flower and clip off the excess.

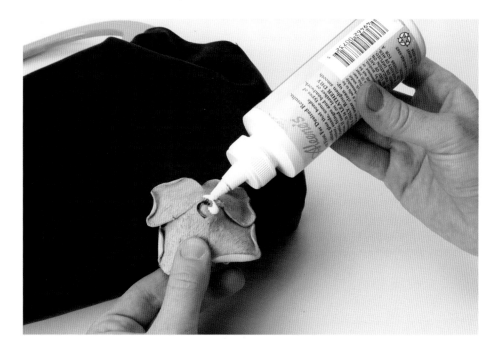

12. Glue the leather flower to the bag using leather glue. Lay the bag flat and let the glue dry overnight.

no-sew & embellished bags

Almost any container can be converted into a purse with just a little imagination, and non-traditional materials, such as metal, plastic, and wood, can be fashioned into one-of-a-kind bags and totes with no sewing required.

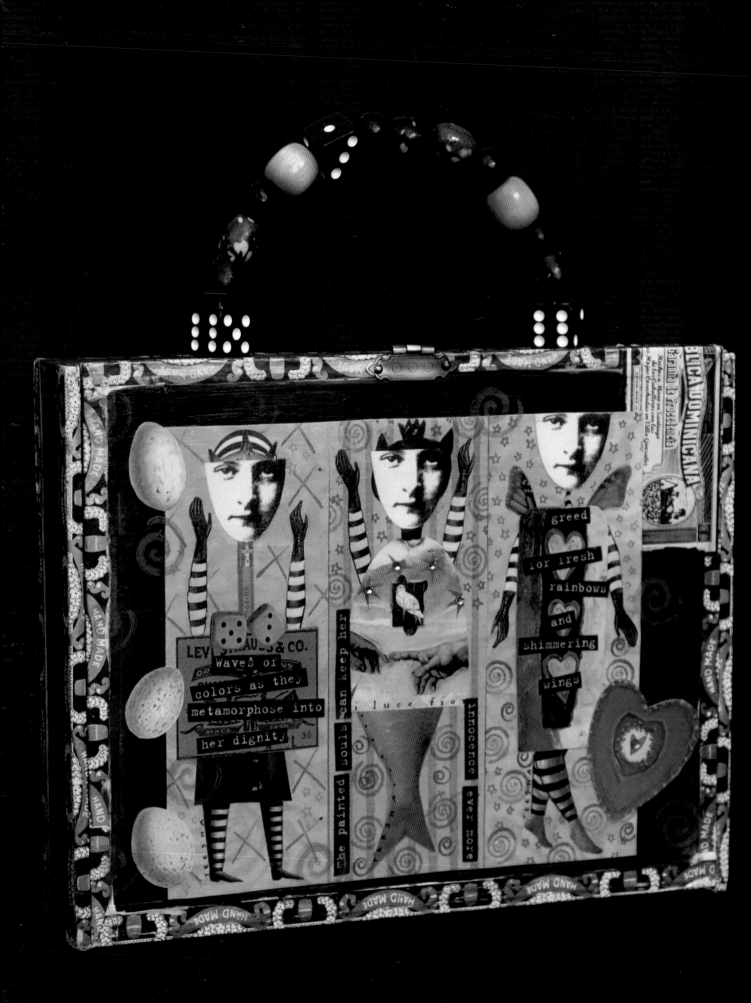

cigar box
purse

Cigar boxes can be purchased from cigar shops or from several sources online. You can find hardware to make them into purses in the home fixtures department of hardware or variety stores. These are funky illustrated purses that are fun to carry during holidays and other special occasions. Add found objects to embellish the design and add dimension and interest to the purse. Try incorporating the color of the box or the original labels into your design.

FOR ONE PURSE, YOU WILL NEED

Empty cigar box

White glue

Sandpaper

Gesso

Acrylic paint

Collage sheets (c28 and c30 from Teesha Moore)

Decoupage glue (Mod Podge)

Rubber stamps

Rubber stamp ink (StazOn™ by Tsukineko®)

9- by 12-inch piece of Quick Stick adhesive-backed felt (CPE)

Craft Hand Drill (Fiskars)

30-inch piece of 20-gauge craft wire

Large wooden beads and dice for handle

Purchased catch or clasp with nails or screws

Rhinestones, glitter, or other small embellishments to decorate box

Gel-type adhesive (E6000)

1. Remove any unwanted labels from the cigar box. A blow dryer can help to soften the glue when removing stubborn labels. Use white glue to repair any tears or to fix loose labels that you want to preserve.

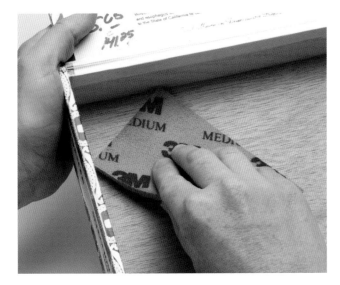

2. Sand rough areas of the wood to remove any burrs or imperfections.

3. If you want to paint your box, brush on a layer of gesso to cover the labels and make a nice base for the paint. Let the gesso dry.

4. Paint the box with acrylic paint and allow it to dry. Leave the inside edges of the lid unpainted as the layer of paint will interfere when closing the box.

5. Cut out and arrange collage images on the front, back, and sides of the box. Brush a layer of decoupage glue on the back of the pieces and glue them to the box. Smooth out any air bubbles with your fingers. Sometimes air bubbles will remain until the paper dries and then will flatten out. Stamp designs on the box with ink if desired.

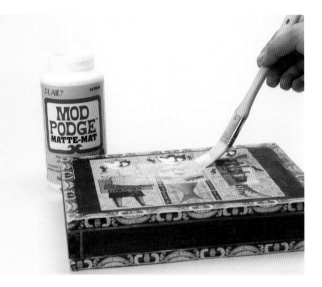

6. Coat the outside of the box with decoupage glue to protect the surface. You can use several coats, letting the box dry thoroughly in between coats. Be sure to follow the manufacturer's instructions.

7. Cut a piece of adhesive-backed felt to fit the inside floor of the box and press into place.

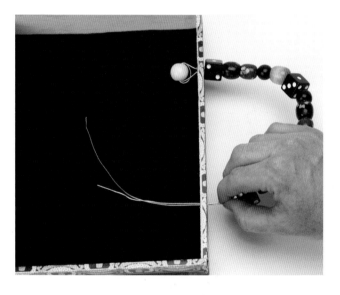

8. Drill two holes in the top end of the box to attach the handle. A manual drill works well for this project. At the same time, pre-drill holes for the purchased metal clasp you will add later on in step 12.

9. To make the handle, thread a bead onto the center of the wire. Loop the wire through the bead a second time for extra security. Twist the wire tightly and run both ends up through the inside of the box through one of the drilled holes. Add beads and dice (the dice can be drilled using a manual drill) to form the handle, threading the beads over both wires. Poke the ends of the wire through the other hole.

no-sew & embellished bags

10. Pull the wires apart to separate them. Add an anchor bead inside the box, threading the wires through opposite sides of the bead. Pull tightly, using pliers to grip the wires if necessary.

11. Wrap the ends of the wires at the base of the bead and clip. Pinch the ends of the wires with pliers to tuck them neatly under the bead.

12. Add a purchased clasp or catch with screws or small nails. If the nails (or screws) extend all the way through, you can rivet or flatten the ends of the nails using the round side of a hammer to tap on an anvil. Embellish the box with flat-backed rhinestones using gel-type adhesive. You can also decorate the box with glitter, sequins, and other found objects.

For these variations I used images from the following sources (clockwise from top): snowy winter box—#IE105 Click-n-Craft® from The Vintage Workshop; collage box—Teesha Moore; butterfly box—antique scrap, *collection of the author; Happy New Year box—photo, collection of the author; Halloween box—Holiday Vignettes CD-ROM and book from Dover Publications.*

clear vinyl
scrapbook tote

If you like hardware, this is the tote for you. There is no sewing or gluing involved; instead, sheets of vinyl are fastened together with metal eyelets. The tote can be made using personal photos, magazine pictures, old record jackets or anything else that can be layered between sheets of clear vinyl.

1. Trim two photos for the front and back panels to measuring 10½ by 7 inches. Apply adhesive sheet to the back of each photo image.

FOR ONE 12- BY 8-INCH PURSE, YOU WILL NEED

Two 10½- by 7-inch photo images

Two sheets 11- by 17-inch double-sided adhesive (PEELnSTICK by Therm O Web)

Three sheets 12- by 12-inch cotton fabric paper (Retro Rocket Rascals by Michael Miller Memories)

Rotary cutter or craft knife

Cardboard or chipboard (10½ by 2 inches)

⅓ yard 54-inch-wide clear, heavyweight vinyl

Hole punch (standard or ¼ inch)

Forty-six ⅛-inch silver eyelets (Prym Dritz)

Four ⅜-inch silver grommets (Prym Dritz)

Eyelet setter

Hammer

Eyelet-setting mat

Grommet setter

Two 1½-foot lengths of chain

Two 1½-foot lengths of plastic tubing

Split rings or key rings (the last three items are available at hardware stores)

2. Peel the protective paper away and press the photo onto the wrong side of the fabric paper.

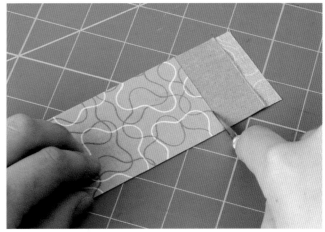

3. Trim the fabric paper around the edge of the photo image with a rotary cutter or craft knife.

4. To make the bottom panel, use an adhesive sheet to attach fabric paper (right side out) to both sides of the cardboard strip. Trim the fabric paper to match the edges of the cardboard.

5. Fold the vinyl in half and cut an 18- by 12-inch rectangle through both layers to make two pieces. Leave the pieces layered together. Set aside. Cut two 9- by 3-inch pieces for the sides. You can do this in one cutting if the vinyl is layered. Peel the pieces apart after cutting as the sides will require only one layer of vinyl each. Cut square notches, about ⅜ inch on each side, at the bottom corners on both side pieces.

6. Place the large layered sheets for the body of the purse over a cutting mat with gridlines. Use a permanent marker to make marks for the eyelet holes along the long sides of the tote. Starting ½ inch from each end, make a mark every inch (about ⅜ inch in from the cut edge of the vinyl). You will have eighteen marks along each side. Match the short edge of one side panel to the edge of the marked vinyl, centering it over the middle two markings. Using a hole punch, punch holes through three layers of vinyl at each mark. Place eyelets into the holes and hammer into place with an eyelet setter.

7. Add the bottom support to the center of the purse: Slip the bottom fabric panel (10½- by 2-inch piece) in between the vinyl layers of the purse body, centering the short end of the fabric panel against the eyelets. Move to the opposite end and set the corresponding eyelets, trapping the fabric base between the layers of vinyl. Attach the remaining side panel as you did in step 6.

8. Form the corners of the tote by matching the side panels with the body piece. Use both hands to press the vinyl together as you form the corner (the clipped corners on the bottom of the panel will help form neat corners). Punch a hole at the next mark through all three layers (after the corner) and set an eyelet in place. Continue punching holes and setting eyelets up one side, keeping all three layers of vinyl together. Move to the corresponding side of the opposite edge of the tote and repeat the same process to form the other side of the tote. Punch holes and set eyelets to attach the sides to complete the tote form.

9. Slip the finished front and back photo panels between the vinyl layers at the top opening on each side.

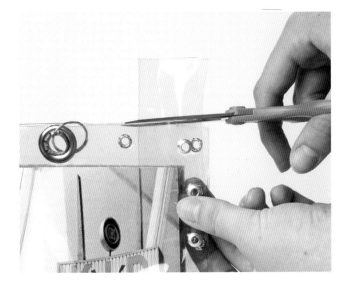

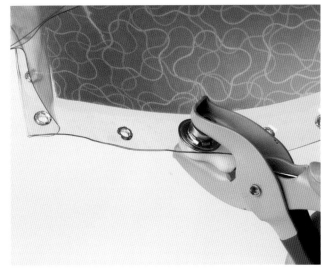

10. Trim away the excess vinyl extending over the top edge.

11. To make handles, mark and punch two large holes on each side for large grommets. The punch will help you to start the hole; use small scissors to enlarge. Set large grommets into place using grommet pliers or a hand setter.

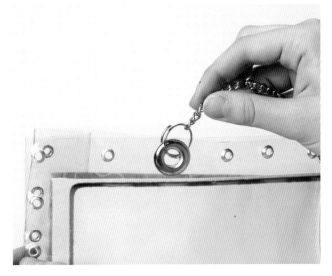

12. Thread a piece of chain through each length of tubing. Use a piece of wire to help pull the chain through the tubing. It helps if the tubing is cold.

13. Attach the chain handles to the tote using split rings to connect the chain to the grommets.

victorian candy tin
purse

Metal is an unusual material to use for a purse, but it works very well to create a fun, nostalgic accessory. Colorful candy and cookie tins are readily available in a variety of shapes. Look for hinged or tightly fitting lids. As an alternative project, try an old tin lunchbox. They are highly collectable and are the perfect container to recycle into a sturdy purse.

FOR ONE PURSE, YOU WILL NEED

Empty candy tin with lid

Decoupage glue (Mod Podge)

Paper to decorate the tin (Paper Reflections® Collage Papers by DMD)

Two ¹/₈-inch eyelets

¹/₈-inch metal punch (Harbor Freight Tools)

Hammer, eyelet setter, and mat

36-inch chain for handle

Two large plastic beads

18-inch piece of 20-gauge craft wire

Wire cutters

Small beads and sequins for decoration (optional)

Gel-type adhesive (E6000)

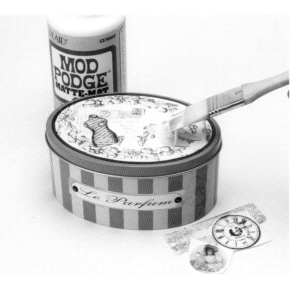

1. Cut out images and attach them to the tin using decoupage glue. Stickers can also be used to decorate the box. Brush a layer of glue over the paper to protect the surface.

2. Use a metal punch to punch a ⅛-inch hole on each side of the tin for the chain handle.

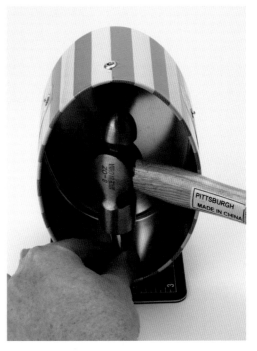

3. Place an eyelet into the hole on each side.

4. Use a hammer and eyelet setter to set each eyelet in place. Hammer the back side of the eyelet inside the tin.

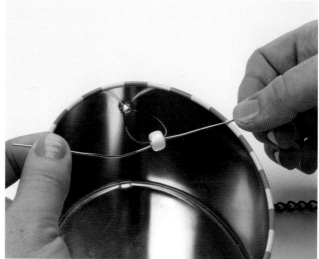

5. To attach the chain handle, thread a small piece of wire through the end of the chain and then through the eyelet on one side of the tin.

6. On the inside of the tin, run the ends of the wires through opposite sides of a large bead, pulling tightly to secure.

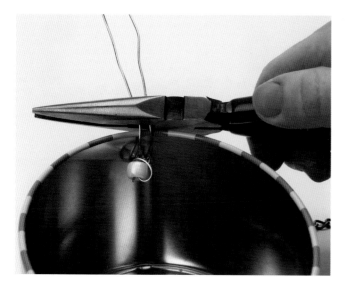

7. Wrap the ends of the wires under the bead and clip off the excess wire. Repeat the process to attach the opposite end of the chain to the other side of the tin. If desired, embellish the tin further by gluing on sequins, small beads, or glitter.

no-sew & embellished bags

polymer clay _purse_

Whimsical purses made by covering a small candy tin with polymer clay are perfect for carrying small change and lipstick for a night out. These purses also make a great package for a small gift. The recipient will be delighted to have a package that is a gift in and of itself.

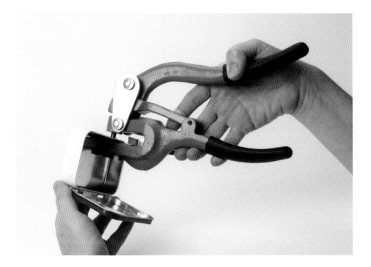

1. Punch two holes for the handle at the top of the bottom half of the tin, ¾ to 1 inch from each side.

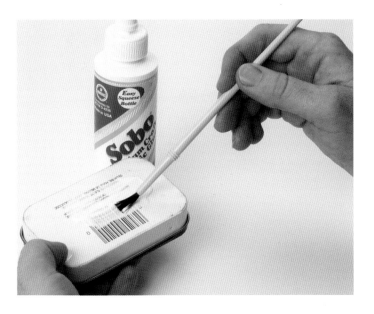

FOR ONE PURSE, YOU WILL NEED

Candy tin with a hinged lid

Metal hole punch

400-grit or medium-grit sandpaper

2 to 3 ounces red polymer clay (Premo™)

1 ounce white polymer clay (Premo)

1 ounce black polymer clay (Premo)

Pasta roller dedicated for clay use

Craft knife

Rubber stamps (#35-183-H by Teesha Moore)

Black ink pad (StazOn)

Glass rhinestones

White glue (Sobo)

Translucent Liquid Sculpey™ (TLS)

Nylon-coated jewelry wire

Two crimp beads

Assorted beads for handle

2. Prepare the tin by lightly sanding it to give the surface a "tooth" for the glue and polymer clay to adhere to. Brush the bottom of the tin with a layer of white glue. Let the glue dry.

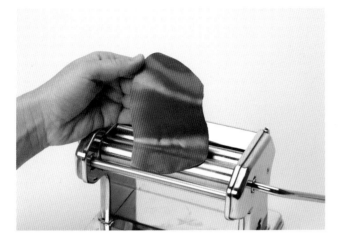

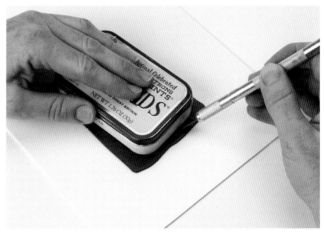

3. Using a pasta roller in which #1 is the thickest setting, roll out a sheet of conditioned (see box below) red polymer clay on setting #4.

4. Place the bottom of the tin on the sheet of clay and press down. Trim the clay along the edge of the tin with a craft knife.

POLYMER CLAY

Polymer clay is a colorful, oven-curing clay that is made of particles of polyvinyl chloride (PVC), to which a plasticizer has been added to make the material flexible. In addition to all colors of the rainbow, polymer clay comes in metallic gold, silver, bronze, and pearl. There are also translucent and liquid forms of polymer clay. It can be modified to imitate stone, ivory, glass, or metal, and images can be transferred to it.

Polymer clay must be conditioned by kneading it with your hands until soft. After conditioning the clay, you can sculpt, roll, or shape it any way you like. Pasta rollers produce nice even sheets of clay in varying thicknesses. All tools used with polymer clay should be dedicated for that use only. Polymer clay should not come into contact with any food-handling items.

To cure polymer clay, bake it on a glass baking dish, ceramic tile, or clean piece of plain white paper placed on a baking pan or cookie sheet. The paper will prevent shiny spots from forming on the clay. Most polymer clay brands can be baked at 275°F for 30 minutes. Polymer clay emits toxic fumes if fired above the temperature given by the manufacturer. Baking fuses the clay particles into a durable plastic.

5. Measure the height of the bottom half of the tin (including the thickness of the clay on the bottom) and cut strips of clay to cover the sides.

6. Wrap the strips around the sides of the bottom half of the tin.

7. Smooth the seams of the clay, joining the sides to the base by pressing the clay strip to the base around the tin.

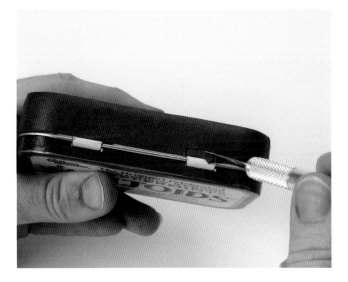

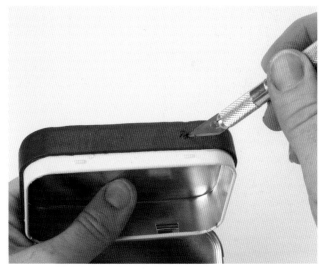

8. Use a craft knife to cut the clay away from around the hinge. This will allow the hinge on the finished purse to move freely.

9. Use the knife to cut through the clay to reveal the punched holes at the top of the tin. Bake the tin on a piece of paper placed on a glass baking sheet or tile. Bake at 275°F for 10 minutes. Let the tin cool. Coat the top half of the tin with glue and cover with a base of clay following steps 3 through 8.

no-sew & embellished bags

10. To make a stamped decoration for the front of the purse, first roll out a thin sheet of white clay (#5 on the pasta roller). Place the sheet on a baking tile and stamp an image onto the clay.

11. Trim the clay around the image. Press glass rhinestones into the clay to decorate. Bake at 275°F for 10 minutes; let the clay cool.

12. Score the back of the baked clay image lightly with a knife. Brush a bit of Translucent Liquid Sculpey on the back of the scored clay and press it onto the surface of the unbaked clay on the tin.

13. To make a striped pattern for the sides and to decorate the surface, roll out a sheet of white clay and a sheet of black clay on the thickest setting (#1 on the pasta roller). Cut the sheets into equal rectangle shapes and stack. Cut and stack again, repeating until you have several layers of clay. Slice off thin sections from the striped "loaf," about 1/16 inch thick.

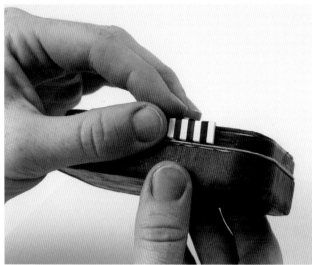

14. Cut small strips of black and white striped clay to decorate the stamped image. Use Translucent Liquid Sculpey to attach strips and frame the baked clay image.

15. Measure the height of the sides of the top of the tin. Cut small sections of black and white striped clay to press around the tin to cover the sides. Cut away the clay from around the hinge as in step 8. Bake the entire tin again at 275°F for 30 minutes. Let the tin cool.

16. To make a handle, cut off a 36-inch piece of nylon-coated jewelry wire. Thread the wire through one of the holes in the top of the tin, bringing the end of the wire to the inside of the tin. Thread on a large bead (larger than the hole) and a crimp bead to the end of the wire. Use pliers to "smash" and secure the crimp bead onto the wire.

17. String beads onto the wire until you are pleased with the length of the handle. Bring the end through the other hole and finish with a large bead and crimp bead. Clip off excess wire.

no-sew & embellished bags

shimmering leaves
purse

You can make your own patterns and designs with rubber stamps and acrylic paints on plain canvas or suede. Lumiere® brand paints are highly pigmented acrylic paints that work especially well on dark fabrics. The iridescent quality of the paint gives the finished purse a rich look that changes with the angle of the light.

1. Use a sponge brush to apply an even layer of paint to a leaf-patterned stamp.

FOR ONE PURSE, YOU WILL NEED

Purchased blank suede or canvas purse

Leaf stamp (Rubber Stampede®)

Emerald green acrylic paint (Lumiere by Jacquard)

Sponge brush

Metal clasp with hook

Head pin

Round-nose pliers and wire cutters

Large bead, small brass bead, and seed bead

Two large jump rings

Jewel or gem glue

Gold polymer clay (Premo)

Bird stamp (Uptown Rubber Stamps)

Black ink pad (StazOn)

Bright copper metallic rub-on paste (National Artcraft Co.)

Hand drill or pin vise

Key chain

2. Stamp a random pattern onto the surface of the purse. Let the paint dry and set according to the manufacturer's instructions.

no-sew & embellished bags

3. For a beaded embellishment, add a seed bead, small brass bead, and a large glass bead to a head pin. Use round-nose pliers to form a loop at the end of the head pin and wrap the wire around the base of the loop. Clip off the excess wire. Use pliers to attach the beaded wire to the metal clasp with a large jump ring.

4. Glue the clasp to the bag with jewel glue.

5. To make a key chain, roll out a thick sheet of gold clay with a plastic roller or smooth drinking glass. Stamp a bird image onto the unbaked clay with black ink. Cut around the outline of the bird with a knife and bake the clay on a smooth tile or glass baking sheet at 275°F for 30 minutes. Let the clay cool.

6. Add highlights to the bird with metallic rub-on paste. Use a hand drill or pin vise to drill a small hole into the wing of the bird. Attach a jump ring and hang the bird from a key chain. Attach the chain to the strap of the purse.

comic appliqué
bag

Decorating a purchased purse blank with iron-on appliqués is a quick and easy way to create a unique design. Cut images from novelty fabrics and arrange them on the bag with trims and buttons. For a truly one-of-a-kind bag, transfer your own images onto fabric using an ink jet printer and paper-backed fabric made especially for printers. Use fabric paints to add color and jazz up your images.

FOR ONE BAG, YOU WILL NEED

One black twill purse blank with handle tabs (Bag Boutique)

U-shaped black handles (Bag Boutique)

¼ yard novelty fabric (Drama Queen by Michael Miller Fabrics)

HeatnBond Lite Iron-on Adhesive

Red rickrack (1 yard or enough to fit around top of purse)

Fabric glue

Large red button

Gem or jewel glue

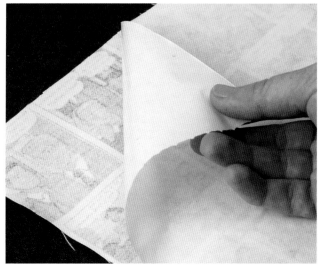

1. Iron adhesive to the wrong side of the novelty fabric following the manufacturer's instructions.

2. Peel off the backing.

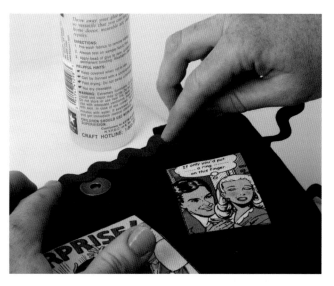

3. Cut out comic shapes from the fabric and arrange on the bag. Iron the images onto the bag following the manufacturer's instructions.

4. Use fabric glue to attach rickrack around the top edge of the bag.

5. Attach handles to the button tabs.

6. Glue a large button for decoration onto the front of the bag using gem glue.

DESIGNING WITH IMAGES

Decorating handbags with images is a fun way to create unique, personalized accessories. Copyright-free images can be found from a number of sources. Dover Publications carries books and CD-ROMs of copyright-free images organized by subject. There are ephemera collections and sources on the Internet for vintage images. Look through your own collection of old books, recipes, and photos to find images that can be copied and used to embellish handbags.

Color copiers, scanners, photo-manipulation software, and ink jet printers enable you to size, retouch, and print images to your exact specifications. You can use photo transfer papers to print an image with your ink jet printer and apply it to fabric, leather, wood, or any other porous surface.

The basic supplies for working with fabric images are a good pair of sewing scissors and adhesive. You can use an adhesive that bonds with heat or you can apply a thin layer of fabric glue to attach fabric images to a purse or bag.

Think about the style of the piece you are making when choosing images to use. If the piece you are designing involves multiple images, you may want to choose images that follow a theme or mix them up for a more eclectic look. You can also combine multiple images into a collage.

no-sew & embellished bags

garden collage
purse

Collage is an expressive art form that has found increasing popularity through altered books, artist trading cards, and fine art. A blank purse is the perfect canvas to combine art images, found objects, and art mediums to make an artistic collage-style purse.

FOR ONE PURSE, YOU WILL NEED

White canvas purse blank (Petit Zip Top Purse by BagWorks™)

Adhesive-backed fabric (Delta FabriCraft™ Peel 'n' Stick Nurturing Garden Designer Pack)

Fabric flowers

Small brass ladybug stamping

Flat-backed rhinestones

Gem or jewel glue

Dimensional fabric paint

Glitter

Seed beads and bits of wire

Plastic alphabet letter beads

Floss or cord

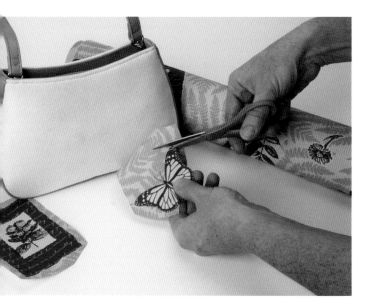

1. Cut out butterfly and floral shapes from the adhesive-backed fabric. Peel off the protective backing to reveal the adhesive.

2. Press the fabric shapes onto the surface of the purse and use gem or jewel glue to attach small embellishments to decorate the purse.

3. Use fabric paint to decorate the butterfly and sprinkle glitter onto the wet paint to add sparkle. Glue rhinestones onto the butterfly with gem glue. Make antennae for the butterfly from a small piece of wire. Bend the wire into a V-shape. Add seed beads to the ends of the wire and bend the wire around the beads. Attach the antennae to the butterfly on the purse with gem or jewel glue.

4. Thread letter beads onto cord, knotting between each bead. Glue the letters onto the purse with gem glue.

no-sew & embellished bags

"altered book"
purse

This is one case where you do want to judge a book by its cover. For this project, look for old cloth-bound books with sturdy covers. Some books have illustrations on the cover that will add personality for a great retro-style purse.

FOR ONE PURSE, YOU WILL NEED

Old cloth-bound book

Craft knife

½ yard cotton fabric

Strip of chipboard or cardboard

1 yard woven belting or cord for handles (cut in half to make a strap for each side)

Large buttons and grosgrain ribbon for decoration (optional)

White glue (Sobo)

Gem or jewel glue

1. Make a paper pattern for the fabric sides of the purse. Measure the height of the text block (inside pages) for the length. Measure the width of the pages for the bottom dimension of the pattern. Make the top of the pattern about 4 inches wide, or wide enough to allow the purse to open. Add a ½-inch seam allowance around the sides and bottom. (Do not add the allowance to the top edge of the pattern as it will be placed on the fold of the fabric.) Set the pattern aside.

2. Use a craft knife to cut the block of text out of the book. Be sure to work carefully to leave the cover intact.

3. Fold the fabric in half with the wrong sides together. Place the paper pattern with the top edge at the fold. Cut two pieces of fabric following the pattern (one for each side of the book).

no-sew & embellished bags

4. Stitch the three open sides together close to the edge on each piece (stitch using a machine or by hand).

5. Clip the bottom corners of each piece to make two notches about ⅜ inch on each side.

6. Glue the bottom stitched edge on the end of the spine inside the open book using white glue. Repeat on the other side.

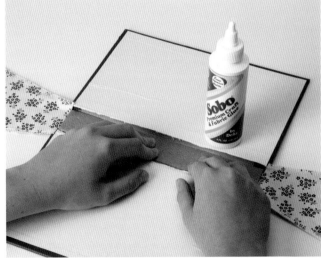

7. Cut a strip of cardboard or chipboard slightly smaller than the inside dimensions of the spine to add support. Glue the strip into the spine, covering the bottom edges of the fabric.

8. Measure the inside dimensions of the book cover and cut a piece of fabric to match. Press the edges under about ¼ inch. Make sure the fabric fits the inside when you fold up the sides of the book cover. The edges of the fabric should not extend beyond the edges of the book. Adjust as necessary.

9. Center the lining fabric over the inside of the cover with the right side up. Attach the fabric to the center of the cover, gluing the fabric edges to each end of the cardboard spine.

10. Flip the loose fabric back and glue straps or cord to the inside of the cover on each side. Let the glue dry.

no-sew & embellished bags

11. Glue the fabric sides of the purse (along the edge of the fabric only) to the inside edge of the book cover.

12. Use office clips to hold the fabric in place while the glue dries.

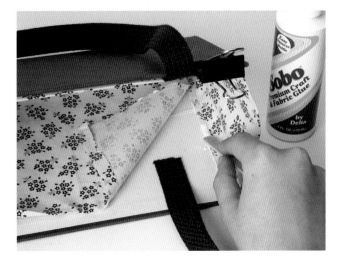

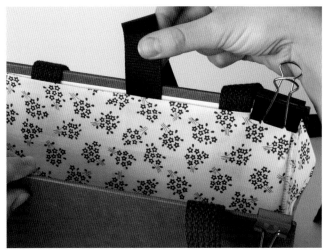

13. Glue the side edges of the lining inside the purse, covering the glued edges of the fabric side panels. Use a wooden stick to apply the glue in tight areas.

14. To decorate the purse, glue one end of a piece of grosgrain ribbon, cut long enough to wrap around the purse, under the lining at the top of the purse.

15. Glue the top edge of the lining in place over the straps and ribbon, leaving a space unglued to insert the other end of the ribbon.

16. Wrap the ribbon around the book, adding a bit of glue to tack it in place.

17. Use clips to hold the top and ribbon in place while the glue dries.

18. Use gem glue to attach a button to the front of the purse for decoration.

pop art
handbag

Take a favorite photo of a friend, a relative, or a pet and turn it into pop art to display on your handbag. The basic idea is to turn an image into a stencil. A great way to make a stencil with an adhesive backing is to use a Xyron® machine. With this machine, you roll a standard 8½- by 11-inch sheet of paper through a cartridge that applies a layer of adhesive to the back of the paper. The paper is then ready to cut and apply to a surface to use as a stencil.

FOR ONE HANDBAG, YOU WILL NEED

Blank black handbag (Kelly Handbag by Bag Works; the other bag in the photo is the Jill Bag)

Photo paper for the printer

Small scissors or craft knife

White acrylic paint

Fabric medium (Delta Ceramcoat®)

Xyron machine with adhesive cartridge

Stencil brush

1. Use photo software to convert a photo into a black-and-white, high-contrast image. Enlarge the image to fit horizontally onto a sheet of 8½- by 11-inch paper. Print the image on photo-quality paper.

no-sew & embellished bags

2. Roll the paper through a Xyron machine to apply adhesive to the back of the image following the manufacturer's instructions.

3. Use small scissors or a knife to cut away the white areas of the paper to create a stencil of the image. You can choose to cut away the black areas instead of the white if you want a negative image. If there are any "islands," or shapes that are not connected, leave "bridges" of white paper to keep the design intact. These can be removed later.

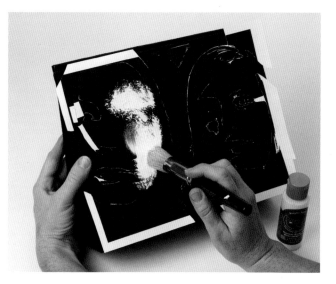

4. Carefully peel the protective paper from the back of the image to reveal the adhesive. Apply the image to the front of the bag, making sure all surfaces are adhered. Clip away "bridges" of paper after positioning unattached "island" pieces into place.

5. Mix white acrylic paint with textile medium and use a stencil brush to pounce or stipple the paint onto the stencil. It's better to stencil two light coats of paint rather than one heavy one. Let the paint dry. Peel away the paper to finish.

polka dot
clutch

Simple and classic in design, this Chanel-inspired purse will always be in style. You can personalize your purse using monogram charms found in the scrapbooking section of the craft store.

FOR ONE PURSE, YOU WILL NEED

Purse form (Shortcut to Style's Classic Clutch from The Vintage Workshop)

One sheet fabric paper (Paris Group from Michael Miller Memories)

One double-sided adhesive sheet (PEELnSTICK)

12-inch piece of 1-inch-wide grosgrain ribbon

Small piece of craft wire

Metal charm with a hole for hanging

Two large jump rings

Fray Check

White glue (Sobo)

Gem or jewel glue

36-inch (or desired length) chain for handle (available in hardware stores)

Two split rings

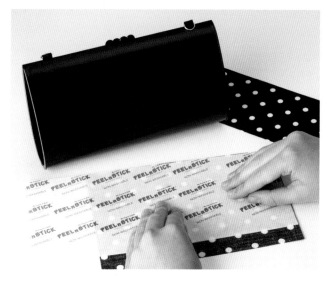

1. Cut two pieces of fabric paper, one for the front of the purse and one for the back. Cut the pieces slightly larger than the surface area of the purse panels. Cut two pieces of adhesive sheet to back the fabric paper. Peel the protective paper from one side of the adhesive and press it onto the wrong side of the fabric paper. Repeat the process for the other cut fabric piece.

2. Trim the adhesive-backed fabric paper to fit one panel of the purse. Remove the backing to expose the adhesive. Press the fabric paper to the purse panel, starting at one corner of the panel and matching the edges.

3. Press with your hand to make sure the fabric is adhered. Cover the other side of the purse.

4. To make a bow, cut a piece of ribbon 8 to 10 inches long and fold it into thirds to form the loops of the bow. Pinch the sides of the bow into the center.

5. Wrap the center of the bow with wire. Twist the wire and clip off the excess.

6. Cut a small, skinny piece of ribbon for the center of the bow. Finish the edges with Fray Check or use a skinny piece of purchased ribbon. Wrap the ribbon around the center of the bow, gluing the piece in place over the wire. Use a clip to hold the ribbon as the glue dries.

7. Add a jump ring to a charm using pliers. Use another jump ring to link the charm and the bow. Attach the bow to the front of the purse using gem or jewel glue. Prop up the purse to keep it level as the glue dries. Let the glue dry overnight.

8. Use split rings to attach the chain for a handle.

no-sew & embellished bags

suppliers

Listed below are the manufacturers and suppliers of many of the materials used in this book. Most of these companies sell their products to retail and online stores. Contact these companies directly to find a retailer near you.

Aspen Art Stamps
P.O. Box 1038
Springville, UT 84663
www.aspenartstamps.com
Unmounted rubber stamps, collage sheets, and vintage milk paint

BagWorks™, Inc.
800-365-7423
www.bagworks.com
Bags, handles, hardware, and kits

Cartwright's Sequins
11108 North Highway 348
Mountainburg, AR 72946
www.ccartwright.com
Sequins and vintage buttons

CPE (Consumer Products Enterprises)
541 Buffalo West Springs Highway
Union, SC 29379
800-327-0059
www.cpe-felt.com
Quick Stick adhesive-backed felt

Delta®
1-800-423-4135
www.deltacrafts.com
FabriCraft™ Peel 'n' Stick adhesive-backed fabric, Rubber Stampede® rubber stamps, acrylic paints, fabric paints, and fabric medium

DMD Industries, Inc.
2300 South Old Missouri Road
Springdale, AR 72764
www.dmdind.com
Paper Reflections® Collage Papers

Dover Publications
31 East 2nd Street
Mineola, NY 11501-3852
www.doverpublications.com
Clip art books and CD-ROMs and copyright-free illustrations

Fiskars®
7811 West Stewart Avenue
Wausau, WI 54401
800-500-4849
www.fiskars.com
Craft Hand Drill

Harbor Freight Tools
3491 Mission Oaks Boulevard
Camarillo, CA 93011
800-444-3353
www.harborfreight.com
Hardware, tools, and metal punches

Jacquard Products/Rupert Gibbon & Spider Inc.
P.O. Box 425
Healdsburg, CA 95448
800-442-0455
www.jacquardproducts.com
Lumiere® and Neopaque® paints

The Leather Factory
P.O. Box 791
Fort Worth, TX 76101
800-433-3201
www.tandyleather.com
Leather, leather-stamping tools, findings, and leather cord

Michael Miller Fabrics/Michael Miller Memories
118 West 22nd Street
New York, NY 10011
212-704-0774
www.michaelmillerfabrics.com
Fabrics and fabric paper

National Artcraft Co.
7996 Darrow Road
Twinsburg, OH 44087
888-937-2723
www.nationalartcraft.com
Art and craft supplies, metallic rub-on pastes, and decorator chalks

Plaid Enterprises, Inc.
1-800-842-4197
www.plaidonline.com
Mod Podge® decoupage glue

Polyform Products Co.
1901 Estes Avenue
Elk Grove Village, IL 60007
847-427-0020
www.sculpey.com
Sculpey™ and Premo™ clay products

Prym-Dritz Corporation
P.O. Box 5028
Spartanburg, SC 29304
www.dritz.com
Bag Boutique™ handbags, handles, and hardware; grommets, eyelets, and sewing notions

Teesha Moore
Box 3329
Renton, WA 98056
www.teeshamoore.com
Collage sheets, rubber stamps, and stamping supplies

Therm O Web
770 Glenn Avenue
Wheeling, IL 60090
847-520-5200
www.thermoweb.com
HeatnBond® Iron-on Adhesive and PEELnSTICK™ Double-Sided Adhesive sheets and tape

Tsukineko®
17640 NE 65th Street
Redmond, WA 98052
800-769-6633
www.tsukineko.com
Rubber-stamping supplies and StazOn™ ink

Uptown Design Company
1000 Town Center, Suite 1
Browns Point, WA 98422
253-925-1234
www.uptowndesign.com
Uptown Rubber Stamps

The Vintage Workshop
P.O. Box 30237
Kansas City, MO 64112
913-648-2700
www.thevintageworkshop.com
Click-n-Craft® CD-ROMs, downloadable art, ink jet printable fabrics and papers, and Shortcut to Style products

XYRON®
7400 East Tierra Buena Lane
Scottsdale, AZ 85260
800-793-3523
www.xyron.com
Xyron machines and supplies

index